The *Ultimate* Curtain Book

The
Ultimate
Curtain Book

A Comprehensive Guide to Creating Your Own Window Treatments

Isabella Forbes

Reader's Digest

The Reader's Digest Association, Inc.
Pleasantville, New York/Montreal

For William and Celia

The Ultimate Curtain Book

A Reader's Digest Book

Designed and edited by Conran Octopus Limited

The acknowledgments that appear on page 192 are hereby made a part of this copyright page.

Library of Congress Cataloging in Publication Data
Forbes, Isabella.
   [Complete curtain book]
   The ultimate curtain book : a comprehensive guide to creating your own window treatments / Isabella Forbes.
     p. cm.
   British ed. published in 1993 under title: The complete curtain book.
   Includes bibliographical references and index.
   ISBN 0-89577-622-7
   1. Drapery. 2. Window shades. I. Title.
TT390.F67 1994
746.9′4—dc20   94-22199

Printed in Hong Kong

Introduction 7

CHAPTER 1   *First steps*

Practical considerations 10
Shapes and sizes 12

CHAPTER 2   *Inspiration*

Entry halls and staircases 24
Living rooms 26
Studies and workrooms 30
Kitchens and dining rooms 32
Bedrooms 38
Children's rooms 43
Bathrooms 44

CHAPTER 3   *Fabrics*

Cottons and linen 48
Sheer fabrics 64
Silks and damask 68
Velvets and tapestry 72
Trimmings 76
Fabric glossary 80

Contents

CHAPTER 4 *Projects*

Measuring 86

Unlined curtains 90

Lined curtains 92

Interlined curtains 94

Headings 96

Valances 108

Cornices 120

Swags 126

Reefing 134

No-sew curtains 136

Tiebacks 138

Roller shades 143

Roman shades 146

Balloon shades 150

Paint effects 154

Finishing touches 158

CHAPTER 5 *Fitting*

Tools and accessories 166

Fitting poles, valance shelves, and rods 168

Poles 170

Rods 174

Fitting shades and reefed curtains 176

Hanging and training 177

Sewing techniques 178

Calculating yardages 184

Care and maintenance 185

Glossary 186

Select bibliography 188

Index 189

Acknowledgments 192

introduction

CURTAIN MAKING IS A SKILL that once acquired gives lasting pleasure. Many are now discovering that it is possible to produce simple, elegant curtains and drapes with the basic sewing skills. With perseverance, the amateur can often aspire to match the handiwork of the professional. Many effects are easy to achieve, others are intricate and challenging. This book aims to provide a comprehensive guide to the entire process of curtain making, from inspiration to the final fitting. It sets out all the options, from the humble roller shade to elaborate confections of swags and cascades, explaining how each is selected, measured, made, and fitted.

The opening chapter gives practical advice on appropriate treatments for different styles of windows and the circumstances that may determine the reader's choice of treatment. In the inspirational chapter that follows, the book looks at how others have dealt with particular rooms, offering ideas for the reader to adapt. Chapter Three provides an illustrated inventory of fabrics with advice on how each is best displayed. Then comes Chapter Four, the practical chapter: here are 35 projects, each with easy-to-follow illustrations and helpful step-by-step information, which show precisely how to make and fit a myriad of different styles and variations of cornices, curtains, shades, and trimmings. A breakdown of the tools and techniques necessary for successful measuring, hanging, and fitting comes in Chapter Five. Finally, there is a section on the principal sewing techniques, a glossary of the main curtain-making terms, and advice on care and maintenance showing you how to insure long life for your curtains.

CHAPTER 1

TIME SPENT IN PREPARATION IS NEVER WASTED.
STARTING WITH THE RIGHT PRACTICAL AND STYLISTIC
CONSIDERATIONS HELPS AVOID COSTLY MISTAKES AND
INSURES A SUCCESSFUL OUTCOME EVERY TIME.

first steps

IT IS IMPORTANT TO START ANY NEW PROJECT with the right spirit, and armed with the knowledge of what's practical. For example, will a curtain style date quickly? Will a treatment insulate the room or mask too much of the window? Does the design complement the period of the house or the rest of the decoration? What are suitable combinations of colors and patterns, fabrics and trimmings? Will certain colors and fabrics fade in the sunlight? Just as important to consider are the different window shapes, each of which suggests a number of approaches. You also need to consider whether to use a cornice, valance, shade, or blinds. Familiarity with all the available options leads to window treatments that are both imaginative and efficient. For a really successful result, always make these decisions before the first selvage is snipped.

A curtain scheme should be sympathetic to its surroundings as well
as the window shape. Formality is appropriate for this early
nineteenth-century town house.

Practical Considerations

A window that opens inward (RIGHT) needs curtains that will not obstruct it. Here a double solution is found. For decoration, the area around the window is swathed in a length of flowered material – making use of a convenient pipe that runs along the wall above the window. In contrast to the busy floral pattern, plain lace curtains are gathered and attached to the window frame then wrapped around the flowered "curtains," to function as tiebacks.

Time spent in contemplation is never wasted when planning new decorating schemes. Following a few basic guidelines will insure that the best – and longest lasting – choices are made.

STYLE AND FASHION

Style is a principal consideration, achieved by a subtle balance between fashion, period, personal taste, and practicalities.

To a greater or lesser extent we are all the victims of fashion, and a lack of funds to realize each passing craze is, in the long run, a boon. The pendulum of fashion is never still. All styles will eventually date and, in time, will find their way into fashion history. Your own preferences will last longer.

PERIOD

Decorative style and architectural period are inextricably linked whether you are decorating a country house or a town house. It is dangerous to pronounce on the wisdom of mixing periods – this must always be a matter of judgment. The lover of Victoriana, living in a red brick nineteenth-century row house, might swag the windows in heavy, velvet drapes. But others might strip away the dark wallpaper, paint the walls in pale shades of honey and cream, and dress the windows in the simplest calico or homespun. Equally, a judicious use of grandiose effects can turn a featureless modern apartment into a palace.

To make a success of any arrangement requires panache and consistency: swags hang uncomfortably at informal windows while frilly chintzes are inappropriate among streamlined modern furniture.

ROOMS

Is the room to be used more often during the day or evening? Does it matter if sunlight is excluded during the day – or is it more important to achieve a grand effect at night? Think carefully about the special characteristics of each room and its use before making any decision about its curtains.

Living rooms used during the day, particularly if east- or north-facing, cannot afford any loss of light from voluminous drapes at the window. By contrast, heavy curtains in dark fabrics will come into their own in a dining room or formal living room used mainly at night.

A draft is often more noticeable when you are sitting still, so a thick interlining inside the lining of curtains is valuable.

A bedroom should be cozy at night and look fresh when you wake in the morning.

A bathroom requires a treatment that is unaffected by steam, can be removed for cleaning, and pulls clear of splashes.

Likewise, a kitchen needs a treatment that is easy to clean and will not retain cooking smells or moisture from steam.

LIGHT

Consider how much light will be blocked at all hours of the day. To preview your curtain effect, mock up the scheme in paper or hang sheets at the window.

HEAT

Curtains can play a vital part in keeping a room warm or cool according to the season. Thick, lined, floor-length curtains help retain heat as well as keeping out drafts.

PRIVACY AND OUTLOOK

Lace curtains are one means of blocking the public's gaze – curtains and shades in sheer fabrics are another alternative. Or consider a pair of stationary drapes with deep folds, which will leave only a small part of the window exposed.

COLOR

Although color is a highly subjective and complex issue, some basic principles should be observed.

Treat a cold, north- or east-facing room kindly with warm, muted colors and soft textures. West- or south-facing rooms can bear the colder blues and grays.

If you do not feel confident about choosing colors, the easiest color schemes are simple and pale and based on just two colors like blue and yellow or pink and green. Aim for consistency, avoiding violent changes of mood, color, or style between rooms.

CHOOSING FABRICS

Follow these three golden rules:
1. Never buy on the basis of a tiny swatch; look at a large piece in situ.
2. Inspect the fabric in natural light.
3. Never think of the window in isolation but as part of the decorating scheme.

CLEANING AND MAINTENANCE

Expert cleaning is a very expensive business. If your curtains need frequent cleaning, avoid elaborate treatments and pale fabrics.

At a sunny window avoid fabrics that tend to fade or rot. Silks, bright colors, and colored linings are vulnerable.

Shapes and Sizes

Elegant drapes with the most formal of swags (RIGHT) adorn a classic bay window. On this large scale such a treatment is well adapted – the deep swags lend warmth and grandeur, each one balanced by its own set of draperies. An extra set has been made to cover the wall next to the windows, lending greater emphasis to the space. What can be a cold expanse of glass has been turned into a haven of comfort in which to sit and read by the light of a graceful lamp.

BAY WINDOWS

A bay window can be a vehicle for elaborate treatments, usually floor-length.

Draperies

A curtain rod must be bent around the window. For the best results a traverse rod should be fitted professionally. There are bendable rods available, but these can cause problems because the draperies may run unevenly around the corners. It is possible to screw the rod to the window frame but it is then visible and can be unsightly. For a more satisfactory solution, suspend it from a valance shelf. The rod can then be hidden by a cornice, valance, or covered cornice board.

There are two ways of treating the three panels of a bay window – a pair of curtains or drapes can be hung at each section and pulled back with tiebacks (see photograph) or one pair of wide drapes can be drawn back to each side, leaving the window free.

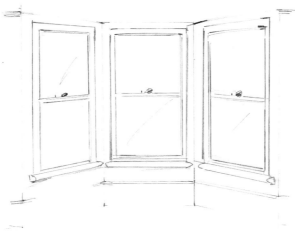

Bay window

Shades

Roman or balloon shades work well on bay windows. The fittings are much simpler than those for curtains and drapes. Window seats don't pose problems, and cording can be carried across the top of the window, to be operated by a single cord.

Roman shades are economical with fabric. They can be painted or stenciled, and any fabric design is shown to best effect.

Balloon shades can be excellent vehicles for trimmings – decorative cording, rosettes, or bows, for example.

BOW WINDOWS

A continuous curve requires a bent curtain rod and a valance shelf cut to fit the shape. Often an inexpensive plastic rod is bent to the curve and fixed to the window frame, remaining visible. This will save money but does little to enhance a pair of draperies. A better solution is to ask either professional fitters or the furnishings department of a large department store to measure, bend, and fit a tailored rod and valance shelf. The rod can be hidden by a cornice, a valance, or a stiffened band of fabric.

The scale of a bow window suggests the use of floor-length draperies. Shades are usually inadvisable since they require a flat wall and window rather than a curve.

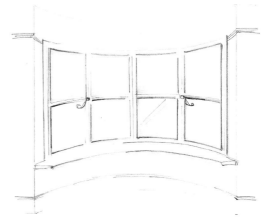

Bow window

SKYLIGHTS

Set at an angle, curtains or shades for sky-lights must be specially adapted to allow for the slope. Generally, the window tilts as it opens and so should not be obstructed.

Special shades are available from the sky-light manufacturers. Alternatively a pole with rings can be fitted above the window using rod sockets. The base of short curtains can then be gathered onto another pole fitted below the window. Long curtains can be pinned back to the wall behind a pole or rod.

For functional purposes a roller shade is most appropriate. When pulled down, it can be held against the wall by cup hooks inserted below the window sill.

DORMER WINDOWS

Dormer windows can present problems, since it is important not to reduce the light yet there is little space for curtains or shades.

One solution is to gather curtains onto swing arms that swivel back against the walls of the recess. Because each side of the curtains will be seen, the main fabric is used on both sides of the curtains.

Alternatively, the outer edge of curtains hung outside the window recess can be cut at an angle and pinned back against the wall using battens screwed into the sloping ceiling. The edge of the curtain is attached to the side edge of the batten using hook-and-loop tape or tacks.

Skylight

Dormer window

Frequently, the simplest treatments are the most effective. In this deeply recessed window (RIGHT), where curtains aren't necessary, a tiny lace valance with a sharply scalloped edge adds a graceful contrast to the rough-hewn walls.

If there is no need to exclude light, a filmy valance of lace or cotton will soften the outline without interfering with the sunlight.

If there is any space above the window, a roller or Roman shade can be used.

A lambrequin – a flat cornice with a shaped outline extending down the sides of the window – provides decorative scope and makes a small window more important. It can be used either alone or with a roller shade.

SMALL WINDOWS

There are two approaches to small windows:
1. Small scale: for a solution that is in scale with the window, try sill-length, gathered curtains or a simple lace valance.

Use a shade inside the window frame if there is room for it. A shade mounted outside the window frame is more flexible but can look strangely detached if the window is deeply recessed.

2. Large scale: try to disguise the modest nature of the window by surrounding it with a cornice and full-length curtains or draperies. In this way the window can be made to appear higher and wider. Take care, however, to avoid too much contrast between window and curtain treatment.

A wide or voluminous shade may make the window appear large when the shade is lowered but, in the raised position, reveal the window as out of scale.

What was once a modest window (BELOW) is now transformed into a major decorative focus with the use of a gilded cornice and full-length curtains. The cornice has been raised to mask as little light as possible and the curtains draw well back to either side for the same reason.

ARCHED WINDOWS

The usual approach to dressing arched windows is to use stationary curtains, cut to follow the line of the arch, either tied back or reefed by means of cords (see page 134). The curtains hang from screw eyes inserted around the curved window frame.

A variation on this treatment is to use a balloon shade (see page 150) cut to the shape of the window, as in the photograph below. These shades will mask light and will not pull up beyond the beginning of the arch's curve.

Another treatment is to use sash curtains (which are gathered top and bottom on rods) for the lower portion, and a fan of fabric, stretched on a custom-bent rod, for the arch.

For curtains which pull back clear of the window, use a pole, either above the window

Here are two contrasting solutions to the same shaped window. In the first (TOP RIGHT), the clean lines of tall, arched windows are complemented by black curtains pinned back to reveal white linings. The black tab headings cut across the arches, which remain as architectural features. The starkness of the design is in keeping with the room's bold, modern feel. In the second (BOTTOM RIGHT), a pair of balloon curtains, cut to follow the window's curved top, use the yielding texture of gathered sheer muslin to soften the view.

Arched window

or cutting across below the semi-circular top. A shade, too, can be hung from a straight fixing but will also cause the arch to be lost or the window to be visually chopped in two.

TALL WINDOWS

A tall and narrow window will look gaunt without a little visual trickery. A cornice or valance, combined with full-length curtains which pull well back to either side of the window, will make it appear wider.

Similarly, a pair of stationary curtains will drape back and frame the view while extending well to either side and lending apparent substance to the window. To avoid revealing bare wall, drape the leading edges over hold-backs on each side.

A charming use of drawn work, a type of embroidery (ABOVE LEFT), serves a practical purpose in diffusing the light while visually breaking up the tall lines of a leaded window. In contrast, slender curtains inside the window recess (ABOVE) and vertically pleated shades (LEFT) emphasize the tallness and narrowness of these windows.

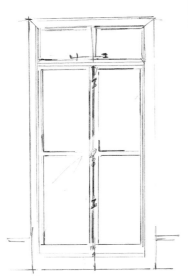

French doors

A pair of checked cotton curtains (RIGHT), hanging from a wood pole, satisfy all the criteria for an informal setting. The lack of valance allows maximum daylight to penetrate and the curtains pull well back to avoid obstructing passage to the patio. Thick interlining inside the lining keeps out heat in summer and cold in winter.

FRENCH DOORS

Some French doors open inward and need a treatment that will not obstruct traffic. This calls for one of three possible solutions:

1. Curtains that pull back to either side, probably hung from a pole.

2. Curtains slotted onto one or two rods that are fixed to the doors themselves.

3. Roller shades, fixed over the glass section of the doors. Roman or balloon shades, even if stacked above the door, are too bulky and would tend to get in the way.

DOUBLE-HUNG WINDOWS

Double-hung windows are receptive to all forms of curtain treatments. These windows are sometimes objects of beauty in themselves, often served more than adequately by a set of contemporary shutters.

A double-hung window will look good with a cornice, valance, or shade. Cornices or valances should be in proportion, and the curtains should be floor-length whenever possible because the sill of this type of window is already so close to the floor.

Double-hung window

Inspired by Scandinavian style, metal arms hold a swag of black-and-white cotton, lined in white. Although the swag seems to be supported only by metal arms, the top is in fact tacked to a board above. For a window without the practical need for curtains or a shade, this simple solution lends interest and a softening touch.

Sliding glass door

PICTURE WINDOWS/SLIDING GLASS DOORS

Often, picture windows are installed to open up a pleasant view that should not then be blocked with curtains. By night, however, the view turns to one of oppressive darkness. Sliding glass doors create the same problem, but there is also the consideration of traffic – people must be able to pass through without obstruction, yet there is often no space to the side for a curtain to be drawn back.

The modern style of so many picture windows and sliding glass doors works best with sleek draperies or shades. Avoid pretty floral chintzes, ruffles, or gathers.

A hard upholstered cornice, with a shaped lower edge and accompanied by a single curtain, is one option for sliding glass doors. However, cornices may look unbalanced without a pair of curtains beneath.

Perhaps more successfully, a single curtain – hung from a pole or from a covered cornice board – can stack back to one side of the door, away from the opening side, during the day and can be drawn across at night.

Roman shades are often ideal when there is room above the sliding glass door or picture window to stack the shades. Their clean lines marry very well with those of the door or window.

DOORS

There are generally two reasons for wishing to cover a door:

1. Drafts: these can be excluded by a single, heavy curtain, hung from a rod that is fixed to the door.

2. Light/privacy: a curtain, its top and base sewn to form pockets, is gathered onto a rod fixed above and below the glass door.

DIFFERENTLY SIZED WINDOWS

Different sizes of curtains, side by side or in the same room, can look clumsy. Try to treat oddly sized windows similarly, finding a compromise solution that will work well for both.

A glass wall (ABOVE) is masked by sheer white muslin. Three solutions to a lack of space by a window are shown here: unity of color disguises a lack of symmetry (ABOVE RIGHT), small curtains (RIGHT) are positioned inside the window recess, and swing arms carry curtains away from a dormer window (FAR RIGHT).

RADIATOR OR WINDOW SEAT

Floor-length curtains will block a radiator's heat and cannot be closed over a window seat. Sill-length curtains overcome these problems but are often visually inadequate – Roman or balloon shades may be better.

To achieve the effect of curtains with the practical advantages of shades, you could combine full-length curtains or drapes, tied permanently back, with a set of roller or Roman shades behind the curtains.

SHUTTERS

Interior louvered shutters fitted on the lower portion of a window look good with a simple valance above the window.

SHELVES OR WALL TO ONE SIDE

Use either a single curtain hung from a pole and swept back to one side, or a roller, Roman, or balloon shade.

INACCESSIBLE WINDOWS

If a window is too high for a curtain or shade to be within reach, a simple cornice or a lambrequin (a flat, shaped cornice extending down the sides of the window) would be suitable as decoration. If light is to be excluded, a shade operated by cords hanging well below the window is a practical solution.

CHAPTER 2

FROM ENTRY HALL TO LIVING ROOM, FROM CHILD'S
BEDROOM TO KITCHEN, A ROOM-BY-ROOM STUDY OF
HOW OTHERS HAVE CREATED THEIR OWN SCHEMES
PROVIDES A RICH SOURCE OF INSPIRATION.

inspiration

*INSPIRATION IS THE STARTING POINT for any project, and
the first step is often the hardest. The choices available
are limitless – for so too is the scope for creativity.
Spurs for the imagination abound, from Federal
town houses to Pennsylvania Dutch farmhouses.
But often the best approach is the simplest, and existing
furnishings and decoration will
help to clarify the options. Don't be
afraid to borrow; see what others have
done and then adapt it to suit your
own individual circumstances. Remember
that simpler and cheaper options will
often work as well as the most extravagant.
This chapter sets out some of the possibilities,
from the humble to the grand, offering suggestions
for every room in the house. Use the treatments for
inspiration, not as gospel truths. A personal flavor is
a vital element in any scheme.*

This imaginative effect is easily achieved. The hard sculpted ridges
of the scallop shells that decorate the tiebacks serve as a foil to the
soft drapes of the cream silk curtain.

Entry Halls and Staircases

A heavy, lined curtain (RIGHT), positioned across an opening, will stop drafts from whistling through the house. These curtains are both functional and decorative, their jewel colors set off by golden walls and polished wood floorboards.

First impressions of a house are often made from the entry hall and center stairway, so effort and imagination here will not go unrewarded. It is not always essential to close curtains at night – and on staircases it is not always possible or practical – so grand or theatrical effects are not restricted by practicality. Windows can be dressed in a myriad of ways, from little lace valances to deep velvet drapes.

Door curtains profit from well-draped hems as an effective aid to insulation. Drawn back to one side along a wood pole, this curtain (ABOVE LEFT) mimics the warm color of the studded front door and keeps out of the way of passing traffic.

Practical considerations can be waived for a staircase window, as in these examples, where frivolous knotted swags (LEFT) and an antique lambrequin (ABOVE) can find suitable settings.

Living Rooms

White walls, plenty of space, and a selected range of glorious colors (BELOW) allow this flamboyant living room scheme to work. The delicate gilded serpents and vivid fringed drapery vie for attention with the elaborate wedding-cake cornice and bold abstract art.

Maximum effort and expense are generally laid out on a living room or family room. Whether comfort or elegance is the priority, these are the curtains or shades that have to be lived with the longest; they deserve careful planning. Often the largest windows in the house are located in the living room, which gives scope for the most interesting and formal treatments. Make sure the rest of the decorating scheme complements the window treatment; the furniture, walls, and flooring should form a satisfying whole, to be enjoyed for years to come.

Regency England's fantasies of the Orient were the starting points for this flight of fancy (LEFT). Gold and jade green drapes, with a dramatic tasseled valance and lilac walls, unite in an explosion of exotic decoration.

Juxtaposing ornamental Indian embroidery with a swagged valance (ABOVE) turns convention on its head but produces a surprisingly successful result. Formal striped bows punctuate the swags, while elegantly draped curtains are complemented by a set of Venetian blinds. The rich colors and shapes of the hand sewn embroidery are highlighted in the sunlight, and the intricate leaves and flowers of the banner, each finished with a tiny bobble, are seen to full effect.

Two matching pairs of heavy curtains (RIGHT) are draped back to frame an enchanting garden view. The simple gathered headings are decorated with central tassels and hung from handsome wood poles, in keeping with the room's elegance.

Simple stenciling turns a plain cornice into a suitably chic companion to a pair of lustrous curtains (RIGHT). Painting a cornice is rewarding while requiring little technical skill. Stencils can be either purchased ready-made or cut out of special stencil paper; any color can then be mixed and applied to a prepared surface. Here circular wreaths – taken from a pair of pillared lamp bases – adorn a flat wooden cornice. Their background is the egg-yolk yellow of the curtains and walls.

This window treatment – more of a hanging that might be found in a contemporary art gallery than a curtain in the traditional sense – is an example of function stripped to its barest minimum. Its part in the overall decorating scheme is vital, providing the principal soft surface and curving shape, in powerful contrast to the stark walls and solid furniture. Its scrolled, black border lends weight and decoration, contrasting with the translucent linen above and emphasizing the airiness of the room itself. The upper corners are sewn with large rings which suspend the curtain from hooks set into the wall. Because of the height of the hooks, a rod, also sewn to the upper corner of the curtain, is necessary for opening and closing.

Kitchens and Dining Rooms

A pair of striped Roman shades (ABOVE) is imaginatively hung from a row of coat hooks, with the cording mechanism operated through screw eyes attached to the top of the window.

Every effort is made to make a small kitchen (RIGHT) appear light and airy. The blue-and-white curtain provides a note of cheerfulness and – when not in use – pulls right back, well out of the way of the sink.

In recent years the kitchen has become an important feature of a house, a room in which much time is spent not just cooking and eating but also talking and visiting. Frequently the kitchen and dining room have merged and the curtains or shades are the focus of quite elaborate schemes. Decorative possibilities know no bounds – from simple checked curtains to theatrical stripes in pink and peppermint.

A wide, narrow window (ABOVE) can seem cold. Here, an improvised valance, in imitation of a balloon shade, filters the light, its graceful loops echoing the elegant sweeps of the wrought iron candelabra.

A glass door (ABOVE LEFT) makes full use of a delicate lace or voile. With pockets at top and bottom, the little curtain is drawn into an hourglass shape, providing the room with an additional decorative touch.

What better use could be made of the small window space above the kitchen sink (LEFT) than as a setting for ranks of charming cups and saucers? An attractive pleated balloon shade provides the ideal opportunity.

In this dining room (ABOVE), reefed curtains (see page 134) pull back in the manner of a toy theater, topped by a wood cut-out cornice of singular design. The striped fabric used for the curtains adds to the cheerful atmosphere.

In a dining room set for Christmas dinner (LEFT) the greens and reds of the textiles and hand-painted walls provide a warm and intimate setting for the festivities. The small, leaded window is made to seem larger and more important with full-length curtains, tiebacks, and a serpentine valance hung with a heavy matching fringe.

Inspired by the aquamarine blues of the Mediterranean, these light striped curtains (ABOVE), with their attached valances, act as a foil to the hard, quarry-tiled floor. Hung from simple iron poles, the curtains are ready to drift in the cool morning breeze but really come into their own in the evening, when they are drawn and the room benefits from additional warmth or softness.

A loop of striped silk, lined in caramel, decorates a window (RIGHT). As the window itself is covered by a shade, the curtain is purely for adornment, its bold shape perfectly in keeping with the pure lines and natural colors of the floor and walls. The sweep of the curtain, in combination with the curving chairs upholstered in lipstick-pink, helps to bring the room to life.

Sometimes a kilim is better as a curtain than as a floorcovering, so that its rich colors and patterns can be admired fully. Here it is used as an ornamental feature, hung from a high pole and draped back, softening the view through French doors.

Exuding the ordered tranquility of a modern cathedral, with its altar-like table and ecclesiastical candlesticks, this room (RIGHT) uses curtains more as an architectural feature than mere soft furnishing. Quilted fabric, hung in orderly folds, covers almost an entire wall – its unusual texture, zigzag rope cording, and burnished steel pole provide a subtle combination of effects. Strong light from a side window enhances the dramatic effect, casting the folds into deep shadow.

Bedrooms

In a bedroom (BELOW) where the pictures and furniture take one back two hundred years, antique shawls and the most delicate sheer muslin curtains seem at one with their surroundings. Practical roller shades are hidden behind the improvised valances.

Much is required of bedroom window treatments. At night they must add to the atmosphere of comfort and tranquility, keeping out light and drafts while giving quiet pleasure and reassurance. By day, and especially first thing in the morning, they need to look bright and cheerful. No other window treatment will be viewed as much – and waking every morning to a badly chosen design or poor workmanship is annoying. The decorative possibilities are endless. Ideally, the curtains or shades should echo some part of the other soft furnishings, if only in a cornice, valance, tieback, or trim.

The simplest of lined curtains, on a gathered heading, are made up in a candy-striped cotton (ABOVE). In a room full of objets d'art and other diversions, they serve their useful purpose without ostentation. The vivid bands of yellow, green, and red are given plenty of room to breathe and bring life to the plain walls and floor.

Asymmetrical drapes across a curtain pole (RIGHT) treat two closely spaced windows as one and lend a suitably masculine atmosphere to this bedroom. With the help of Venetian blinds, the arrangement is both decorative and practical, allowing for the maximum entry or exclusion of light. By day the blinds can be adjusted to allow a discreet view of the outside world or can be drawn up and hidden behind the drapes. By night the blinds drop, their dark wooden slats harmonizing with the polished mahogany dresser. Two candlestick lamps add formality, framed by the blinds.

Nothing frames a garden view more prettily than fresh cotton (ABOVE), strewn with flowers in the colors of a bright spring morning. Here, a pinch-pleated valance, generously in proportion with the full-length draperies, is decorated with covered buttons and accompanied by a matching bedspread. The draperies stack back against the wall on each side of the window, and the valance is hung well above the window space. In this way neither will block daylight and the window is made to seem larger than it really is.

The frame of a campaign bed (RIGHT) stands in contrast to the silk folds of a pretty pull-up curtain. Copied from an eighteenth-century design, it does not fall to floor-length, which would be accurate historically, but instead skims a window seat and radiator.

A roller shade (RIGHT), in a bright gingham check, is visible through sheer curtains, edged in a pompom fringe, turning the tiny dressing room into a haven of tranquility.

A silk curtain (BELOW) is swept back in a grandiose gesture to one side of what is actually a modest-size window. White, creams, and honey colors make a restful background for the filtered morning sun.

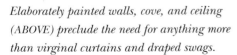
Elaborately painted walls, cove, and ceiling (ABOVE) preclude the need for anything more than virginal curtains and draped swags.

A room (RIGHT) filled with visual interest and diversion, from tented toy cupboards to flying acrobats, features yellow and white tab curtains. The white stripes appear to extend over the back of the blue wood pole and attach to the front with bright coordinating blue buttons.

Blues and terracotta (RIGHT) have always been used together as a happy balance of visual warmth and coolness – here, warm ironstone-colored walls set off the cool blue and white stripes of the Roman shades. With inward opening windows the shades pull up above the window recess to stay well out of the way of rampaging children and allow for a pair of day beds to be placed end to end, discreetly providing extra accommodation by night and a generous-size sofa by day.

Children's Rooms

Our most vivid and lasting memories are acquired in childhood. A nursery curtain or wallpaper motif will often be remembered for life, and should aim to inspire happy memories. When a new baby is born the child's room becomes a focus for the parent's best decorating skills – stenciled bunnies hop around the ceiling, dotted Swiss and floppy bows adorn the window. Whether it is the strictly conventional or the more unusual that appeals, a child's room should both reassure and amuse, developing and changing as the years pass.

None of the furnishings in this light and airy bedroom under the eaves (RIGHT) attempts to compete with the wonderful sights and scents beyond the open window. The simple muslin curtains are loosely held back with narrow tiebacks and topped with a plain valance, all in the same pristine fabric. White cane chairs and white-painted woodwork add to the calm atmosphere.

Childhood fantasies are fuelled by legions of Noah's animals (ABOVE) as they march across wall and shade in a coordinating frieze, wallpaper, and fabric scheme. The roller shade has its wavy lower edge picked out in a contrasting color while a cloud-shaped cornice is adorned with fat blue polka dots. By way of visual relief the area below the chair rail is painted in cool blue-green tones, and a comfortable yellow armchair offers itself as a welcome source of rest to a tired parent.

Bathrooms

While privacy and the steamy atmosphere are the twin considerations when planning a bathroom curtain or shade, there is still scope for invention. The shapes and colors of shells or fishes might provide artistic inspiration; shining chrome faucets and a gleaming enamel bathtub might call for a sleeker, monochrome treatment. Shades are useful here; they can be made in a variety of ways that will let in light without a loss of privacy. Muslins and voiles, too – whether plain, patterned, or fringed – come into their own in such settings.

An exotic yard and a room full of seashells (LEFT) call for the coolest and lightest of natural materials – here provided by caramel-colored rattan blinds and floating sheer muslin curtains with unusual ruffled headings. Tolerant of a humid bathroom atmosphere, they will cater to the most modest bather, excluding the outside world when necessary.

The dramatic sweep of a double-layered curtain of checked cotton and printed voile (ABOVE) lends a note of high drama to this bathroom. Finishing touches include a padded edge and a coordinating sash tieback.

The best solution for any bathroom window is often a neat Roman shade. This one (LEFT), its nautical stripes in keeping with the clean white porcelain and scrubbed wood floor, can be pulled clear of splashes or can be let down for privacy. Lined in a plain, translucent cotton, it still allows sunlight to penetrate.

CHAPTER 3

CHOOSE FROM THE TARTAN OF A SCOTTISH CASTLE TO
THE MUSLINS OF A SCANDINAVIAN INTERIOR, FROM THE
FLORAL CHINTZES OF THE ENGLISH STATELY HOME TO
THE PRINTED SILKS OF THE FRENCH CHÂTEAU.

fabrics

FROM TIME IMMEMORIAL, FABRICS have provided a rich inspiration and medium for designers and artists. Titian's sixteenth-century nudes are set against swags of silks and damasks, the Impressionists turned their vibrant palettes to the design of printed cotton, and, in the 1880s, the Arts and Crafts movement found expression in the patterns of William Morris. Fashion has now come full circle, traditions have endured, and the French brocades and Indian chintzes of two hundred years ago can still be found — at a price. With toiles de Jouy and striped silks vying for attention with luxurious velvets and tapestry, making the right choice is often a bewildering experience. Achieving a happy balance stylistically, while remaining aware of the practical considerations for each type of cloth, is vitally important.

Silk brocades jostle heavy tassels; swirling paisley designs vie with
twisted cords as trimmings are matched with materials in the pursuit
of the perfect decorating scheme.

Cottons and Linen
Checks and stripes

Combinations of checks and stripes in natural materials are currently enjoying considerable vogue. They are inexpensive and easily cared for and can evoke anything from a sunny Swedish farmhouse to a verandah on Cape Cod. Tickings and ginghams look perfect against polished floorboards or pale color-washed walls. Use checks and stripes in coordinating colors for treatments with simple, clean shapes. By combining such patterns with plain cottons, successful schemes can be achieved with ease.

All fabrics cotton unless indicated

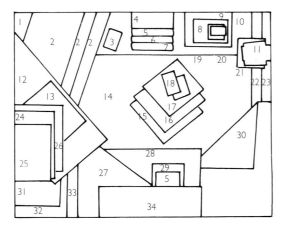

1. Canvas 2. Glazed plain chintz 3. Plain weave 4. Herringbone weave 5–6. Color-woven cotton 7. Herringbone weave 8. Hand-woven rib 9. Printed cotton 10. Indian hand-woven slub 11. Hand-woven cotton 12. Hand-woven slub 13. Gingham 14. Woven check 15. Indian hand-woven slub 16. Woven check 17. Indian hand-woven slub 18. Hand-woven solid rib 19–20. Indian plain rib 21. Natural canvas 22. Glazed plain chintz 23. Woven check 24. Gingham 25. Herringbone weave 26. Indian hand-woven slub 27. Glazed printed chintz 28–30. Indian hand-woven slub 31. Color-woven cotton 32. Plain weave 33. Indian hand-woven slub 34. Indian hand-woven cotton

Lined cotton curtains and a shallow gathered valance lend themselves well to this room (RIGHT). To maximize the daylight, the valance is less than the usual one-fifth of the curtain length, and is set on the outside of the window recess to avoid interfering with the inward-opening windows.

Sunlight filters through a pair of checked gingham curtains (BELOW) looped onto a brass pole with gingham tabs.

Raised by means of two cords set well in from the edges, this window treatment (LEFT) – halfway between a balloon and a Roman shade – retains its straight base with a slat inserted just above the wide lower border.

Two curtain fabrics are used (RIGHT), but the treatment is unified by the colors and the use of ribbons to attach the curtains to the metal pole. Asymmetry and the juxtaposition of pattern and fringe add interest.

Cottons and Linen
Small-scale prints

The South of France has given us a taste for brightly colored Provençal cottons. Vivid hues, like yellow and indigo, evoke a feeling of spring. Gathered into simple treatments for small bedrooms, bathrooms, and kitchens, they look good hanging from a plain brass pole or in a simple gathered valance. Generally made from pure cotton, they are easily washed, regaining their brilliance and crispness.

Discretion is the key word when dealing with small-scale patterns. A tiny floral motif should be matched sympathetically with diminutive windows, using narrow edgings and delicate trimmings, with informally gathered headings taking precedence over formal pleats.

All fabrics cotton unless indicated

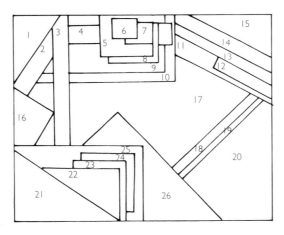

1. Printed cotton 2. Provençal printed percale
3–4. Printed cotton 5. Linen/cotton mixture
6–7. Printed cotton 8. Provençal printed percale
9. Printed cotton 10–11. Glazed plain chintz
12–13. Printed cotton 14. Heavy printed cotton
15–16. Provençal printed percale 17. Printed linen
18. Provençal printed percale 19. Glazed plain chintz
20. Provençal printed percale 21–3. Printed cotton
24–6. Provençal printed percale

Small prints can be used on a large scale (BELOW). The most formal of staircase windows becomes a major decorative focus, and a floral chintz, suggestive of the leafy garden beyond, makes the prettiest possible use of a constricted space. The narrow stripes of wallpaper and roller shade match the curtains in color and scale.

Matching wall coverings to curtains is a fine art. Here an unusual combination of Roman shade and swag in a muted printed linen (ABOVE) is set off against a coordinating fabric wallcovering. What could seem ostentatious in garish colors or fancy finishes is given grace by a unified and restrained choice of designs and colors. Another approach is to merge curtains and walls (BELOW). Done with aplomb – with the floral design lightened by a plentiful pale background color – a grand effect is achieved.

Cottons and Linen
Modern prints

Over the last forty years or so textile design has moved from the mill into the art school, providing a choice between "traditional" and "modern." Here "modern" ranges from the "Grandma Moses" fabrics of the fifties, depicting scenes of rural America, through the Matisse-inspired fashions of the eighties to the classical revival of the early nineties. Blocks of vivid color wrestle with abstract images, Post-Modern "architectural" prints, and Neo-classical motifs with the palm trees of the South of France. Consistency is the key. In the airy spaces of a modern interior, matched to the stark shapes of contemporary furniture, you can show off strong colors against pale surfaces, and combine hard and soft textures in a generous use of fabric, with simple headings and fittings.

All fabrics cotton unless indicated

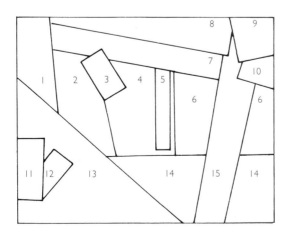

1. Printed sateen 2–3. Printed cotton 4. Sateen and brushed cotton 5. Printed cotton 6–7. Glazed printed chintz 8. Printed cotton 9. Glazed printed chintz 10. Printed cotton 11. Printed stripe 12. Printed cotton 13. Kashmiri embroidery on cotton 14. Glazed printed chintz 15. Printed cotton

A revival of interest in classical engravings has spawned a whole new genre of fabric designs – here (RIGHT) a composition of ruins and mythological figures is cleverly relieved by a bold stripe that intersects the cornice and runs along the leading edges (center, vertical edges) of the draperies. In this way the scenes can be viewed in detail, framed by the coordinating fabric.

Though technically undemanding, both of these treatments (RIGHT and FAR RIGHT) have a greater impact than many a fancy, time-consuming scheme. With such boldly striped fabrics, fussy headings would be superfluous – here, even pleats are dispensed with.

This fresh, modern
scheme (ABOVE) shows
checked gingham in a
whole new light by
utilizing unpleated,
well-stiffened headings
and a cleverly
camouflaged rod on
floor-to-ceiling
windows.

In this more intimate
room (LEFT) a
strikingly patterned
Roman shade is set
against plain velvet
drapes, in a careful
juxtaposition of hot
plum with cool yellow.

Sheer Fabrics
Voiles, lace, and muslin

Translucent fabrics have lately come to be appreciated for the brightness and airy elegance that they lend to a room. Patterns, either woven or printed, are shown off to best advantage as the light penetrates, creating shadows that twist and turn in the curtain's folds. Cottons and silks; muslin, lace, or organza; embroidered, woven, or printed; these fabrics are friends to the light and can find a home at the tiniest dormer window or festooned from the highest ceiling. The freshness given by featherlight fabrics – sometimes backed up by a roller shade – is inestimable. When choosing a sheer fabric, pay attention to the care and maintenance it will need. Ideally, use washable fabrics in natural fibers.

All fabrics cotton unless indicated

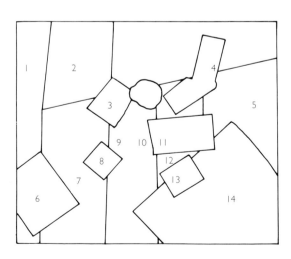

1. Muslin 2. Voile 3. Silk organza 4. Cotton and silk sheer 5. Lace 6. Fine lace 7. Lace 8. Silk organza 9. Self-woven check 10. Dotted Swiss 11. Cotton mix voile 12. Muslin 13. Embroidered cotton 14. Embroidered cotton and silk sheer

A length of antique lace (BELOW) is easily transformed into an exquisite glass curtain by hanging it, unpleated, from a plain wood pole using clip-on rings. In another simple but stunning treatment (RIGHT), a sheer muslin hourglass curtain blends unobtrusively into an all-white decorating scheme.

Color and pattern are by no means the only considerations when planning a scheme. A successful marriage of texture, shape, and space in relation to walls, floor, furniture, and furnishings requires an indefinable, instinctive sensitivity. A fear of straying from conventional, ready-made coordinating fabrics blunts the pleasure of putting together delicious combinations of mossy velvets and crisp linens, silks and delicate voiles, and whitewashed walls. A Scandinavian dining room (CENTER LEFT), all polished and painted wood, the honey-colored floor fading to the palest dove-gray walls, is set off by featherlight muslin curtains. In a similar combination (LEFT) of hard and soft, solid and translucent, the textures emphasized by the strictest range of vanilla and dusty-blue-gray with an improvised valance of knotted muslin, this country family room invites contemplation and tranquility. In a third example (ABOVE), daylight is again used to highlight the glorious feel and color of Indian saris, here used in a highly original – if not strictly practical – manner, permanently draped at a bedroom window.

Silks and Damask

Luxurious silks and damasks have always been highly prized. The manufacture of such cloth dates back to ancient China, Egypt, and Constantinople. France and Italy now lead the field, producing cloth of superb design and quality. However, cheaper equivalents can be found in many fabric stores and there is much fun to be had from combining inky velvets and gleaming silks, and using a little fantasy to concoct exotic treatments. Plain silks can look sumptuous in almost any context, their lustrous finish acting as a foil to dark stained poles and gilded or brass fittings. The traditional patterns of damask designs often provide a useful dimension in the balance between floral, geometric, and plain colors, finding an appropriate place in any curtain scheme.

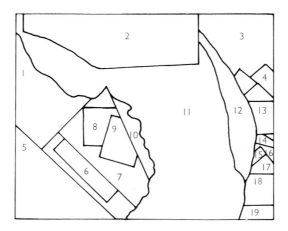

1. Color-woven silk 2. Embroidered silk
3. Embroidered damask 4. Printed silk 5. Color-woven silk 6. Embroidered damask 7. Silk damask
8–9. Printed silk 10. Plain velvet 11. Embroidered silk damask 12. Plain velvet 13. Printed silk 14–17. Plain silk 18. Embroidered viscose with satin finish
19. Moiré silk and embroidery

Early nineteenth-century France is evoked in this room (RIGHT). The furniture, furnishings, and swagged curtains could have come out of a Napoleonic upholsterer's manual. The blue silk decorated with the golden repeated motif is typical of the period, and a gilded pole continues the theme, with the Emperor's laurel wreath as its central focus.

Silks usually make the happiest of companions for tassels and fringing. A simple pair of lined curtains (RIGHT) is given discreet importance with a pair of central tassels. The curtains' hems carry fringe echoing the color of the stripes on the upholstered chair nearby. The green taffeta of a pair of unlined curtains (FAR RIGHT) is lent a decorative touch with matching tassel tiebacks and fringing.

Rich damask, antique embroidery, and a band of beaded velvet give a splendid feeling of opulence to surroundings as varied as a rustic French staircase and the muraled halls of an Italian palazzo. A flat shade (ABOVE LEFT) is a novel use for a rich silk damask but its subdued colors complement the pitted plaster and Delft tiles. An embroidered banner (LEFT) has strayed far from its origins but is clearly much loved. In an eclectic interior full of objets trouvés its unusual position above a staircase seems quite appropriate. Finally, in a setting not short of visual interest (ABOVE), golden silk curtains, each decorated with a pearl-encrusted band, add to the high theatricality of garlanded pomegranates and fantastic pilasters.

Velvets and Tapestry

Setting layers of richly colored, densely woven fabrics together, unified by a basic palette of deep burgundy, forest green, or midnight blue, can create an appealing style that spells both warmth and comfort. The Victorians used such fabrics to great effect, with deeply swagged velvet curtains and tartan-covered walls. Use velvet for heavy fringed curtains, tied back with twisted cord, or try tapestry for a draft-excluding curtain over a doorway. A Gothic-looking deep cornice or lambrequin (shaped flat cornice with long sides), decorated with fringes or cord, will help to create a soft, dark interior.

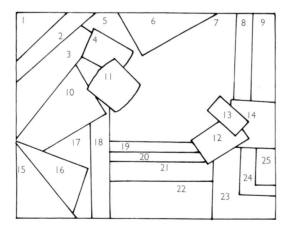

1. Wool and cotton bouclé 2. Cut and uncut velvet 3. Printed cotton velvet 4. Crushed cross-dyed viscose velvet 5. Heavy mohair-mix velvet woven plush 6. Cotton damask 7–9. Printed silk damask 10. Wool and cotton cut bouclé 11. Crushed cross-dyed viscose velvet 12. Linen and cotton mixture 13. Smooth cotton velvet 14. Cut velvet 15. Silk-screened cotton 16. Printed cotton 17. Textured cotton velvet 18. Silk and cotton damask 19. Heavy printed cotton 20. Jacquard 21. Wool and cotton bouclé 22. Cut and uncut bouclé 23. Classic color-woven damask 24. Printed cotton 25. Finely woven wool plaid

A paisley print of midnight blue and deep burgundy (RIGHT) is well suited to the masculine atmosphere of this room. The Arts and Crafts movement favored weighty fabrics decorated in dense botanical prints. In this alcove (BELOW) the greens and ambers of the William Morris textiles look at home against the polished wood paneling.

The dense luxuriance of old-fashioned plush (ABOVE) lends warmth and coziness, both visually and in practice, as it effectively insulates one part of a room from another.

Crimson double-tasseled velvet drapes (RIGHT) create a curvaceous outline that is echoed in the arabesques of the Orient-inspired wallpaper. The rod-pocket heading works surprisingly well here.

A rich pattern is never shown to better effect than on full-length curtains (ABOVE) — and here the excellent draping qualities of a woolen paisley provide a subtle contrast to a bare wood floor and translucent undercurtains.

Trimmings

Trimmings bring an air of luxury to the simplest cottons. Color and scale are the main considerations – a heavy linen swag merits a thick bullion fringe, while an unlined cotton curtain requires something lighter. Many companies produce ranges of color-coordinated fabrics and trimmings, sparing the customer the long hunt for the perfect match – and trimmings can be dyed to match a fabric. Borders and fringes, braids, and welting can be used to add sharp color accents and extra definition, while cords and tassels add movement. Textural contrast adds another dimension – for example, a soft cotton fringe throws the sheen of glazed chintz into relief. Trimmings can also affect proportions: a deep fringe along a cornice will help to stress the horizontal, while a tassel at the center point of draped curtains visually reduces height.

Soft linen fringe in a brindled black and white (LEFT) is a conventional finish for a generous serpentine valance, showing off the curved shape while supplying welcome monochrome relief in a room filled with pattern.

In contrast, a translucent white linen curtain (RIGHT) uses an exotic beaded fringe as decoration, the light highlighting both the fabric and colored glass while passing breezes trigger a delicate tinkling sound.

Border braid (FAR RIGHT) can be used to outline and define the shape of curtains and shades and other decorative details. Used to pick out colors from the room scheme, trimmings can impart a sense of unity to the overall decor.

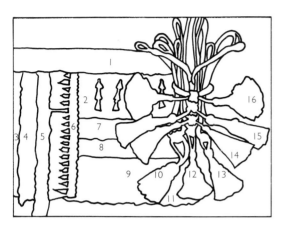

HEAVYWEIGHT TRIMMINGS

1. Viscose tassel fringe 2. Light tassel fringe 3. Viscose fan edging 4. Viscose and cotton frayed fringe 5. Viscose and cotton narrow braid 6. Tufted bullion fringe 7. Viscose and cotton frayed fringe 8. Viscose and cotton broad braid 9. Light tassel fringe 10. Single tassel tieback 11. Heavy tassel fringe 12. Cotton double tassel tieback 13. Viscose and cotton double tassel tieback 14. Cotton tassel tieback 15. Cotton tassel tieback 16. Double tassel tieback

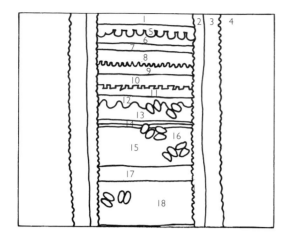

LIGHTWEIGHT TRIMMINGS
1. Linen and cotton bullion fringe 2. Wide cotton fringe 3. Small cotton bullion fringe 4. Scalloped cotton edging 5. Cotton pompom fringe 6. Cotton fringe 7. Linen and cotton fringe 8. Linen and cotton seersucker braid 9. Linen and cotton long fringe 10. Linen fan edging 11. Narrow cotton braid 12. Small cotton fringe 13. Large cotton fringe 14. Cotton braid 15. Wide cotton braid 16. Linen and cotton button tufts 17. Small cotton fringe 18. Large cotton fringe

Fringes and braids can take on a multitude of forms and uses, edging a tieback (ABOVE LEFT) or pinched into rosettes on a scalloped cornice (ABOVE RIGHT). In both cases the colors are coordinated, while the textures soften hard outlines and add interest to basic shapes.

Linen fringe finds a novel home along the top edge of pull-up shades (LEFT), where it echoes the striped theme of wall and fabric.

Translucent cotton curtains (LEFT) are given a decorative air with a two-color pompom fringe. The simplicity of the curtains complements the jade-green walls and patterned floor. The fringe links the principal colors of the room while adding a delicate touch to the sweeping drapery.

Fabric Glossary

The enormous variety of fabrics now available for curtain making – from inexpensive cotton duck and linen-cotton mixes to luminous silks and damasks – offers all manner of decorating possibilities. But no matter how expertly constructed the window treatment, the wrong choice of fabric will mar the end result. Practical considerations – as well as aesthetics – must be kept in mind.

How will it drape? Will it wrinkle? Will it fade in bright sunlight? Will washable fabrics shrink? Try to obtain a sample length to look at – a small swatch can be misleading. Always look at fabric in all lights and be sure to buy enough material; an extra length from new stock may show a noticeable color variation.

Here is a selection of the most commonly used fabric types.

BASIC FIBERS

Cotton The vast majority of furnishing fabrics are made of cotton or cotton mixtures. Its principal charm is its versatility. Cotton can be dyed, printed, or finished in a multitude of ways. It can be made colorfast, will withstand heat and light, and yet is inexpensive. Drawbacks, shared with all natural fabrics, are that it tends to crush and can react to humidity by mildewing.

Silk So far, no artificial fiber can match silk's lustrous surface, its draping quality, or its subtle response to light. However, it may rot faster than other fabrics when exposed to light. If necessary, silk curtains can be protected by a roller shade. Not all silk is expensive: simple, plain-colored silks can come within even modest budgets. Take special care with the maintenance of silk curtains or shades; they should always be dry cleaned. Bear in mind that silk will show water marks.

Linen Linen is made from processed flax which lends the finished fabric unusual strength, so it is a good choice for curtains or shades. Slow to deteriorate and hard-wearing, it also drapes well to give graceful folds. Many fabric companies use linen for their designs.

Wool As a furnishing fabric, wool has few uses. The only major exception is wool tartan, borrowed from the clothing industry for its colors and patterns.

MAN-MADE FIBERS

Acetate Many convincing artificial silks are made from acetate. It has almost the same finish and draping qualities as silk but is less prone to fade or rot.

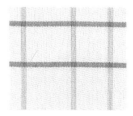

Viscose (rayon) Viscose is the oldest man-made fiber. It adds strength and luster to cotton and silk blends. Its distinctive sheen is used to highlight patterns, particularly in damask.

FABRICS

Baize Dyed green or red, baize is a flannel-like cloth used for card tables and the linings of silverware drawers. Its color and texture make it handy for improvised curtains or shades. Baize will fade in strong sunlight.

Batik In this dyeing process developed in Java, wax and other substances that resist dye are applied, then washed out to leave dramatic patterns.

Eyelet A white cotton fabric, embroidered with open designs, eyelet is very useful for both lightweight curtains and for unlined shades.

Brocade A fine fabric originally made of silk but now produced with man-made fibers. Traditionally patterned with both floral and naturalistic motifs, the raised design is woven on a Jacquard loom and has long horizontal threads along the back.

Cheesecloth A cheap, loose-woven cotton used for translucent curtains. In cities it will quickly lose its original whiteness and body and, although easily washed, muslin will shrink. This fabric also wrinkles badly.

Cotton lawn A finely woven cotton, with a very smooth finish.

Muslin Plain-woven white cotton, varying in weight. Unbleached muslin is off-white.

Canvas A heavy woven/linen cotton mix. See *cotton duck*.

Chintz Plain chintzes are used for contrasting welting, or even as the main fabric. Floral chintzes were originally block-printed, and then glazed with waxes and starch. Gradually the designs developed into the lush floral patterns so closely identified with English country-house style. Chintzes are made from cotton and usually finished with a shiny glaze that is easily lost by crushing or cleaning.

Cotton duck A cream cotton varying in weight from 7 to 15oz per sq yd (200 to 425g per sq m). Heavier varieties are hard to penetrate with a needle and so are ideal for no-sew curtains as they need no lining and the edges can be pinked and glued. Widths range from 36in (91cm) to 134in (340cm). The edges may need trimming.

Crewelwork An Indian cotton fabric decorated with wool chainstitch, usually on a cream background.

Damask Highly traditional, cotton or silk damask is woven with large, abstract leaf and flower designs in contrasting matte and satin textures. It is made on a Jacquard loom, the warp and the weft usually in the same color. Also woven in other mixtures, it is similar to brocade but is flatter and reversible.

Dupion Real or artificial silk with a slubbed, or textured, surface. Real silk dupion is generally imported from India; it is a lightweight fabric which, like other silks, tends to fade and rot. Artificial dupion is made of acetate and viscose.

Gingham A checked cotton fabric which is a perennial favorite cheap and charming furnishing fabric. Gingham comes in a wide range of primary colors and check sizes. The best gingham is made of pure cotton.

Grosgrain A silk cloth with a pronounced ribbed surface.

Holland Medium-weight cloth made from linen or cotton. The non-fraying edges make it ideal for roller shades.

Ikat Chinese silk or cotton fabric tie-dyed to create softly outlined geometric patterns.

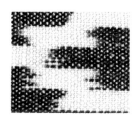

Lace An openwork fabric, usually made of cotton, and useful for glass curtains. Lace designs are almost infinite, from the tiny repeated floral motif to large-scale designs of birds and animals.

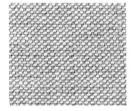

Linen union An inexpensive and hardwearing linen-and-cotton mixture.

Madras cotton Brightly colored fabric, woven with a checked plaid or striped design.

Moiré A watermark effect on silk, now a finish for man-made silk imitations. Water removes the finish.

Muslin lawn A crisper and more finely woven version of cheesecloth. It makes excellent translucent curtains.

Marquisette A thin, open-mesh fabric, often of artificial fibers.

Paisley Fine woolen cloth printed with intricate scroll or pine designs, which have become a classic motif.

Plush Old-fashioned form of velvet, with a deeper but sparser pile. Favored by the Victorians, it was made from wool or mohair and sometimes cotton. The modern equivalent is man-made.

Sateen A strong cotton or cotton-blend fabric, often striped or in a bright solid color, with a smooth, almost shiny, finish and a close weave.

Shantung Unevenly textured raw silk, once hand-woven in China's Shantung province.

Dotted Swiss A sheer fabric with opaque dots which are sometimes flocked to create a raised texture.

Taffeta Fine, crisp silk with a finish that also gives it the name "paper taffeta." It has numerous man-made imitations. It should be treated with care as it wrinkles badly.

Tapestry Now made on a Jacquard loom, woven tapestry fabric was originally produced in imitation of hand-sewn tapestries. It is a heavy fabric and will make a very good insulating curtain.

Tartan A woolen cloth woven with a particular checked pattern of specific colors, each belonging to one of the Scottish clans. Its rich, deep colors can be effective in any interior and it has good insulating qualities.

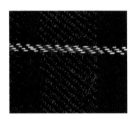

Ticking A striped cotton originally used to cover mattresses. Traditional ticking has narrow black-and-white stripes, but modern tickings come in a range of colors. White downproof ticking is intended for cushion pads but can also be made up into curtains and shades.

Toile de Jouy A cotton or linen fabric printed with scenes of French pastoral life, traditionally in dark red on a cream background. First fashionable in the eighteenth century when it was produced in the French town of Jouy, it can now be found in numerous single colors on a plain background. An effective furnishing fabric, if it is used in moderation.

Tussah silk A raw silk, originally Indian. Not easily dyed, it is typically a yellowy-brown color.

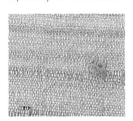

Velvet A cotton fabric (more rarely silk or wool) whose pile gives it a soft surface that absorbs light. Velvet is luxurious but needs careful handling when pressed. Gaufraged velvet has an impressed pattern. Brocade, or façonné, velvet has a burnt-out pattern.

Voile A white translucent fabric, ideally of cotton, to be used behind curtains or as a window dressing in its own right.

LININGS
Cotton sateen Lining comes in various qualities and prices but it is usually a tight-weave fabric called cotton sateen. A more expensive lining will retain its body after cleaning and will help the curtains or shades to hang well. Cheap lining can become limp with age and cleaning. Ivory, cream, and white are the usual basic shades, although lining is now available in a wide range of colors and patterns. If the curtain is to be tied back to show the lining, a coordinated color or pattern should be used. Swags, where the lining is visible, should also be lined in a coordinated design. Colored linings are colorfast but will fade in a sunny window. With patterned linings care should be taken to make sure that the design of the lining will not show through to the right side of lightweight curtains.

Aluminum-coated Without adding much extra bulk, this type of lining will help to exclude light, cold, or heat. It can be used with curtains or, when bulk is particularly unwelcome, to line shades. The aluminum-coated surface faces inside the curtain or shade, while the visible side shows cream-colored woven cotton.

Blackout A layer of opaque material is sandwiched between two layers of cotton fabric. In this way all light is excluded. Some are heavy and difficult to penetrate with a needle, while others are softer. Both will add to the weight but will also improve the draping qualities. Usually in cream or white.

INTERLININGS
Bump This heavy, blanketlike cotton interlining imported from England is available bleached or unbleached. Table felt or reinforced felt is similar but is somewhat stiffer. Cotton flannel can also be used instead of bump. All interlinings are sewn into a curtain between the fabric and lining; lockstitch links the interlining to the curtains. These heavy interlinings can also be used for cornices but are too heavy for swags. They are often too heavy to use with silk or other light fabrics.

Domette Also imported from England, domette is a cotton interlining that is lighter than bump, table felt, reinforced felt, and flannel. Needle-punched fleece is the closest American equivalent to domette. These lightweight interlinings can be used for light curtains, swags, and shades.

Synthetic Usually composed of 85% viscose and 15% polyester, synthetic interlinings are cheaper than the cotton equivalents but lack some of their qualities. They do not have the same softness or body and so will not drape as well. While cotton interlinings will adhere to the curtain fabric, synthetic versions will tend to repel other fabrics and thereby lose fullness. Light penetrates a synthetic interlining more than a cotton one. However, they do not have the weaving faults of cotton interlinings, nor is there the danger of shrinkage. They are clean and easy to handle.

Batting A fluffy man-made fiber sometimes used to pad edges.

STIFFENERS
Fusible heavy-weight buckram An open-weave fabric, made from jute, then impregnated with glue, this type of buckram is used as the base of a cornice. It is very stiff and is best cut with a heavyduty craft knife. A hot iron will release the glue to fuse it in place. It is turned on its side along the cornice.

Non-fusible heavyweight buckram Also made from jute, this material is not impregnated with glue but is double starched and two-ply. It is sewn into the cornice. Again, use a heavyduty craft knife because non-fusible buckram is not easy to cut. It has the same uses as the fusible version but is more easily cleaned.

Non-fusible buckram A medium-weight cotton buckram that will fold well, it is sewn into tiebacks.

Fusible buckram This is a strip of white cotton impregnated with glue. It is used inside hand-pleated headings, giving the requisite stiffness without the visible machine stitching of a sewn-on decorator tape. This buckram is fused to the fabric with a hot iron.

CHAPTER FOUR

THIRTY-FIVE PROJECTS, WITH DETAILED STEP-BY-STEP INSTRUCTIONS ON MAKING EVERY SORT OF CURTAIN, CORNICE, AND SHADE, FROM MEASURING TO VARIATIONS ON A THEME.

projects

TWO CENTURIES AGO IT COULD TAKE the upholsterer's apprentice many years to master the basic skills of curtainmaking. Even today, professionals take great pride in the subtleties of the craft, only fully mastered after long experience at the worktable. Although it is the custom for curtainmakers to swathe the intricacies of their art in mystery, nevertheless, with a thorough knowledge of the basic skills, the mysteries will soon be revealed and confidence gained to tackle ever more ambitious projects. Practice and experimentation will reap dividends – whether you are lining a curtain, trying out a handmade heading, designing a cornice, or painting your own fabric patterns. It is vital to take exceptional care with measurements. Accurate measuring is an important aspect of the upholsterer's art, and time spent in preparation is never wasted.

A green cotton band trim snakes around the edge of a floral chintz curtain, its lively checked lining providing an expert-looking finish.

Measuring
Curtains, Cornices, and Valances

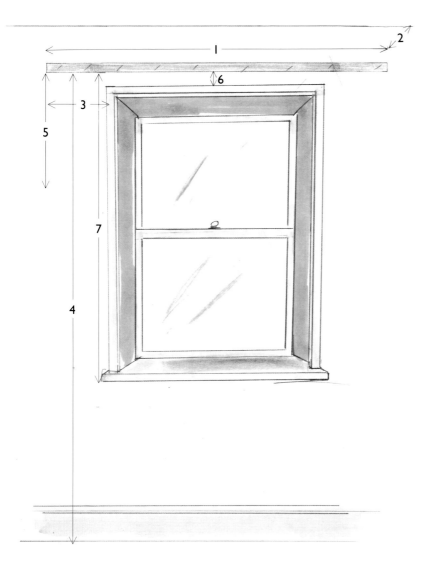

1: Finished width of curtain headings. Add 3in (8cm)
    for overlap
2: Returns: add to width if applicable
3: Space for curtains to stack back
4: Finished length to floor
5: Finished length of cornice – 20–25% of (4)
6: Finished length of sill-length curtains
7: Space between valance shelf and window

Armed with accurate, detailed measurements, you can tackle any new project with confidence. If you are careful, you can avoid unpicking and remaking a lovingly constructed curtain or shade just because a single digit was written down incorrectly.

CURTAIN OPTIONS
❏ First, decide on the length of your curtains. They generally look best if they finish in line with the window or the floor, rather than in between.
❏ Floor-length is often preferable, particularly in a living or dining room where they will emphasize the window, and are needed to balance cornices or valances. Flamboyant arrangements can take draped hems, but avoid them if you are not prepared to arrange the hems every time the curtains are opened or closed.
❏ Shorter curtains – which fall either to, or just below, the windowsill – are suitable for more modest windows, particularly in kitchens and bathrooms.

CURTAIN WIDTH
❏ For finished width, measure the length of the rod, pole, or valance shelf (1), allowing for any returns (2) and enough space

(3) for the curtains to stack back to each side beyond the glass. Allow 3in (8cm) for an overlap where they meet in the center.

CURTAIN LENGTH
❏ For finished length, allow for a ½in (12mm) gap between the top of the curtain and the base of the valance shelf. For covered cornice boards, allow for the heading to run flush with the top of the board. With an exposed rod, allow for the heading to cover it when the curtains are closed.

Floor-length curtains
❏ To graze the floor (4): deduct ¼in (6mm) so they fall just short of the floor.
❏ Draped on the floor (4): add 2–4in (5–10cm) to the finished curtain length.

Sill-length curtains
❏ Try to make the curtains fall just below the sill (6).

Stationary curtains

❑ Measure in the same way as balloon shades (see below), but allow for two curtains that overlap in the center.

❑ The curtains will be hung from screw eyes or hook-and-loop tape along the front edge of the valance shelf.

❑ The overlap should be held in place by a tack or finishing nail. This is often hidden by a rosette or cording; or use a tack and work the head through the front layer of fabric.

Cornice or valance

❑ The depth (5) should be 20–25% of the curtain length, although a serpentine cornice or valance may drop much lower at the sides.

Rod position

❑ The rod will either hang alone, and exposed – in which case it should be positioned just above the window mounted on the wall or the window trim – or be screwed to the base of the valance shelf and hidden.

❑ The distance between the valance shelf and rod and the window (7) can be adjusted to alter the apparent height of the window. The higher the shelf and rod, the taller the window will appear. Be sure not to position the shelf, rod, or pole too high or it will seem out of proportion. If it leaves a section of wall exposed, this can easily be disguised with a cornice or valance.

TIEBACKS

❑ Tiebacks are needed when the curtains are to be draped back from a wholly or partly closed position.

❑ Measure around the curtain at the chosen height, insuring that the tieback doesn't crush the fabric or hang limply away from the leading edge of the curtain.

❑ Allow for welting if required.

❑ Depending on the fabric design, tiebacks can be cut on the straight or the cross grain. Make a pattern and experiment with the most economical use of fabric.

SHADE OPTIONS

See page 88.

❑ When measuring for shades, the main consideration is whether to hang them inside or outside the window opening. Inside is often neater, particularly for Roman or roller shades, but avoid blocking light or impeding the window itself. Shades hung outside the window opening will give greater flexibility in size and can also be used to make the window appear substantially larger.

SHADE WIDTH

❑ Balloon shades (1): to extend along the front of the valance shelf and the returns.

❑ Roman shades (2): to cover the front edge of the shelf, but not the returns.

❑ Roller shades using either a side-winding or spring-roller mechanism may be

Points to remember

❑ Always measure once the fittings are in place.

❑ Make notes and sketches to help recall details. A Polaroid camera can be very helpful.

❑ Use a 16ft (5m) retractable steel tape measure.

❑ Enlist help to hold the tape measure in position.

❑ Use a step ladder to reach the top of the window.

❑ It is vital to insure that all measurements are correct before cutting the fabric. Check every measurement twice.

❑ Make several finished-length measurements since floors can be uneven and windows out of plumb.

❑ Don't forget to add seam and hem allowances to all measurements.

❑ Allow for window seats and sills. Nothing should push against the back of the curtains or shade.

❑ When measuring the width, allow for returns (the distance the rod projects from the wall) if you are using a projecting rod.

❑ On each side of the window, allow about one-sixth of the width of the glass for stackback – the space taken up by the curtains when open.

❑ Don't forget to allow for contrasting fabrics, tiebacks, and welting.

❑ Take the pattern repeat, if any, into account before calculating the yardage requirement (see page 89).

❑ For curtains hung from a track screwed to the valance shelf, measure the finished length from the base of the shelf. Then calculate the hook drop – this will depend on the different configurations of curtain tape and curtain rod. Allow ½in (12mm) clearance between the top edge of the curtain and the base of the shelf.

❑ For curtains hung from a pole, measure from the base of the curtain ring.

❑ For stationary curtains attached to the front and side edges of the shelf, measure from the top of the shelf and add just over an inch (a few centimeters) for the top edge of the curtain to stand up above the shelf.

❑ For a Roman shade, measure the finished length from the top edge of the valance shelf, then add the depth of the hook-and-loop tape – 1in (2.5cm) is enough. This will be run along the top of the shelf, just behind the front edge.

❑ For a balloon shade, measure from the top of the valance shelf and add just over an inch (a few centimeters) for the head to stand up above the shelf.

❑ Allow for seam allowances and hems at the top, bottom, and sides. Different curtains and shades require different dimensions, so always check the instructions.

mounted outside (3) or inside (4) of the window opening. They may be side-, top-, or face-mounted. The pin length (the overall length of the roller fitting) is 1¼in (3.2cm) less than the cloth width. If hung inside the opening, allow for the pin length to be ¼in (6mm) less than the actual width of the opening. In this way there is an ⅛in (3mm) gap between the end of the roller and the wall.

SHADE LENGTH

❑ The hem of a balloon shade should hang 8–12in (20–30cm) below the sill, so that the scallops along the lower edge are still visible when the shade is fully extended (5); or, if it is in effect a full-length curtain, it should be made to graze the floor.

❑ A Roman shade (6) or roller shade (7 & 8) will hang to the sill, or slightly below if the sill does not protrude.

Allow for an extra 10–12in (25–30cm) to be left rolled up at the top of a roller shade, even when down.

YARDAGES FOR SHADES

❑ The flat width (hem measurement) of a balloon shade is two to two-and-a-half times the finished width (heading measurement).

❑ The flat width of a Roman or roller shade is the same as the measured width (see above) plus allowances for top, hem, and side seam allowances. A Roman shade lining should be given extra length to allow for the pleated dowel pockets (see page 146).

SWAGS

❑ Like cornices and valances, swags can be hung from a valance shelf which, when accompanied by curtains, is fitted with a curtain rod beneath.

❑ To work out the dimensions of a swag, hang a chain or piece of covered chain weight tape from each end of the shelf. Adjust to follow the lower curve of the finished swag (1).

❑ The distance along the top of the shelf represents the top edge of the swag (2).

❑ To assess fabric quantity, cut out a pattern in the correct shape with (1) as the base edge, (2) as the top edge, and a depth (4) two to two-and-a-half times the pleated depth (3). Allow for cutting the swag on the cross grain for plain

fabrics. Fabrics with an obvious pattern or with a noticeable nap, which cannot be tilted to a 45° angle, must be cut on the straight grain.

❑ The inside edge of the cascades (the fabric hanging down at each side) should be the same depth as the actual swag (3), i.e. the central draped portion of fabric.

❑ The outside edge of the cascades should be half the length of the curtains (5).

❑ The width requirement for cascades varies, depending on the type selected. The best solution is to cut a (paper) pattern for the cascade, pleat it up, and work out the dimensions. The cascade in the project for Silk Swag and Cascade (see page 128) requires seven times the finished width, plus the return, plus a 2in (5cm) flap which will curl around the inner edge.

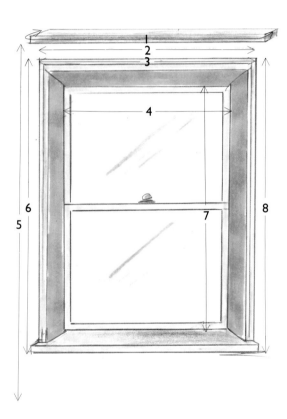

1: Balloon: finished width
2: Roman shade: width
3: Roller shade outside opening: width
4: Roller shade inside opening: width
5: Balloon shade: finished length
6: Roman shade: length to sill
7: Roller shade inside opening: length
8: Roller shade outside opening: length

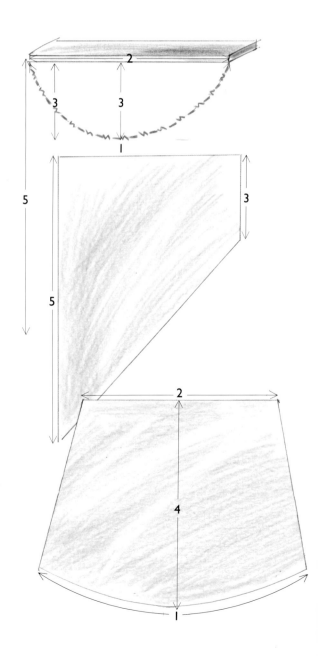

MATCHING PATTERNS

❑ Patterned fabrics have what is known as a "repeat." This is the vertical distance between each section of repeated pattern. Establish the size of the repeat before buying or cutting the fabric.

❑ When the pattern is matched horizontally, the calculations required for figuring out yardages are straightforward. Work out how many repeats you will need to cut to fit into the required cut length of fabric. For example, if a repeat is 24in (61cm) and the cut length needs to be 79in (2m), four repeats – 96in (2.4m) – will need to be cut each time. It is necessary to cut more than is needed to avoid cutting a different part of the pattern with each length. There will often be waste, particularly with large repeats (a).

❑ Less easy are the fabrics with a half length repeat. When laid side by side, the pattern does not match horizontally and the fabric has to be extended by one-half of a repeat so that the

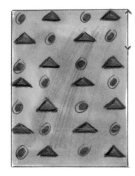
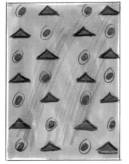 **a**

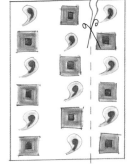

c

pattern abutting the selvage coincides horizontally. One whole extra repeat should be added to the number of repeats calculated above since one-half of a repeat will be lost at the top and bottom of joined lengths. Bear this in mind, too, when making a pair of curtains. The pattern should run across a pair of curtains when closed (b).

❑ To avoid having to cut off a whole repeat each time, it is possible to cut a section of

pattern off the side of a length. In this way, the next vertical section of pattern will match the adjoining length without having to raise or lower the fabric. However, you lose width with this solution (c).

❑ To match a pattern accurately, use a ladderstitch to baste seams prior to stitching them (see page 179).

❑ Few patterns are printed in a perfect horizontal. Be prepared to follow the pattern in favor of the strict grain of the fabric.

Before you start

❑ Before you start, check the whole length of fabric for flaws and quantity.

❑ Check all calculations and measure out the lengths carefully before cutting.

❑ Cut a small piece of fabric across the top corner of each length – then you will always know which is the top and which is the bottom.

❑ As each length is cut, fold it carefully and put it to one side, or roll it back onto the cardboard tube to avoid wrinkling or damaging the glaze.

❑ Buy plenty of fabric in the first place. Different dye lots can vary greatly.

❑ Buy lining in the same width as the face fabric: the seams will then coincide.

❑ Match thread carefully to the fabric for both color and fiber. Large projects will need more than a single spool.

❑ If weights are difficult to obtain, use coins.

❑ Make sure that the machine needle is sharp – blunt needles will pull threads. Keep a good stock of needles and pins.

❑ A soft pin cushion and a thimble are important aids to good sewing.

❑ Have plenty of clear workspace, and keep threads and needles orderly. Time can be wasted searching for lost scissors or pin cushions.

❑ Tidy up at the end of each day. It is much easier to start with everything in its place.

❑ Make sure to have a good light source in your work area.

❑ Keep hands clean.

❑ Avoid leaving cups of tea or coffee where they can be spilled.

❑ An extension cord is helpful for the iron and sewing machine.

❑ Beware of melting nylon carpets with the iron if you are working on the floor. Use a folded piece of cloth as protection.

❑ Avoid overfilling the steam iron – unwanted splashes on fabric can be disastrous.

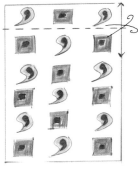
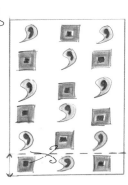
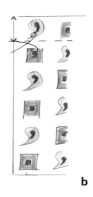 **b**

Unlined Curtains

MATERIALS
Face fabric
Strip of stiffener (for handmade heading) or tape (for stitched heading)
Weights or covered chain weights

Unlined cotton curtains (BELOW) gently filter sunlight.

Unlined curtains can provide a gentle, translucent finish to a window, softening – but not excluding – daylight. Like any other curtain, they can have pinch-pleated, pencil-pleated, or gathered headings (either machine-stitched or handmade) and look best with delicate trimmings.

Making unlined curtains is an excellent project for those inexperienced in the art of curtainmaking, and the quick and effective results that can be achieved provide the encouragement needed to try something a little more challenging next time.

If the curtains are to be washed, it is advisable to pre-shrink the fabric and use pre-shrunk tape, and also to leave a generous lower hem that can be let down at a later date. Watch out for handmade headings: stiffeners like buckram, particularly the fusible type, are difficult to clean.

MEASURING
❑ Width: The flat width should be two-and-a-half times the finished width. Add 2in (5cm) for side hems.
❑ Length: Add 4in (10cm) to the finished length for the hem. Add 3in (7.5cm) for a machine-stitched heading, 8in (20cm) or 6in (15cm) for a 4in (10cm) or 3in (7.5cm) handmade heading.

MAKING UP
1. Cut the widths of face fabric.
2. Join the widths using French or flat-fell seams (see page 181).
3. Turn under ½in (12mm) then another ½in (12mm) along side edges to make double hems. Slip stitch leaving 10in (25cm) at the top and bottom.
4. Turn under a double 2in (5cm) hem at the bottom. Lace or sheer curtains can be stitched close to the fold.
5. It is advisable to insert weights into unlined curtains, especially when they are floor length. Covered chain weight tape, inserted into the fold of the hem, and hand sewn at corners and seams, is suitable for lightweight curtains and will help to anchor the curtain to the floor without being visible against the light (a).

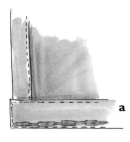

6. Alternatively, for a heavier fabric, prepare standard weights by sewing them into small lining fabric bags (b).

7. Miter the lower corners, and then sew the bags into the miters at the base of each vertical seamline. Pin, baste, and slip stitch close to fold (c).

8. An unlined curtain can have either handmade headings, stiffened with a strip of buckram, or machine-stitched tapes attached to the back of the curtain. Fusible buckram is impregnated with glue that is released by a hot iron, thus attaching it to the rest of the curtain. Non-fusible buckram (see page 83) has to be handsewn into the heading. Handmade headings are hand-pleated, while machine-stitched tapes are drawn up on cords or pleated with hooks.

Handmade heading
1. Cut stiffener to the flat width of the curtain.
2. Place the strip flush with the top edge of the fabric, on the back,

under the side hems. Baste in place (d).

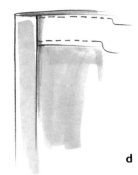

3. Fold the stiffener and fabric over twice to encase stiffener.
4. Slip stitch along the base and up the sides of the heading (e).

5. If using fusible buckram, remove the basting and press the heading with a hot iron to release the glue in the buckram, which then holds the heading in position.
6. The basting stitches and slip stitches will hold non-fusible buckram in place.
7. To pleat the handmade heading, see page 97.

Machine-stitched heading
1. Turn under 3in (7.5cm) at the top. Lay the tape along the back of the curtain. Pin, baste, and stitch. Hold the heading taut while stitching, and make

sure that both rows of stitches start from the same side of the curtain to prevent puckering. If using corded tape, trap the cords with stitches on the leading edge, and leave them free on the outer edge. As the heading is pulled up to its finished width, the cords will be pulled out to one side only. The cords can be knotted and hidden behind the curtain (f & g).

2. If a narrow decorator tape is used and the heading is visible, not hidden behind a cornice or valance, the tape should be lowered by at least 2in (5cm), forming a ruffle above the tape (h & i).
3. Wider tapes should always be positioned ¼in (6mm) down from the top edge. When calculating the finished length of the curtains, allow for the distance

between the hooks and the top edge.

HANGING
Handmade heading
Attach pin-on or sew-on hooks to the back of the heading (see page 98).

Machine-stitched heading
1. If using corded tape, pull the cords in the tape to the desired width, forming even pleats. Excess cord should never be cut, but should be looped up and hidden behind the curtain. When the curtains are washed or cleaned the cords can simply be untied.
2. Insert the hooks into the pockets in the tape. If using uncorded tape, the pleater hooks form the pinch pleats as the prongs are pinched together.
3. There is usually no need to "train" unlined curtains since they are unlikely to have enough body to form uniform pleats.

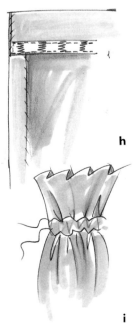

Lined Curtains

Simple lined curtains are the best solution in a wide variety of situations. They are simple to make and, depending on the lining, can be light and billowing or protect against drafts and sunlight. In addition to conserving energy and making a room more comfortable, linings protect curtains, helping them to last longer. Blackout linings are also available, which block out light completely. Yet another benefit of linings is the uniform appearance they give curtains from outside the home. And, of course, they add body; even a simple cotton lining will give curtains and drapes more substance.

The techniques involved in making a simple lined curtain are easy to master and are an excellent way to familiarize yourself with basic curtainmaking skills.

Washing lined curtains is not advisable, as the main fabric (known as the face fabric) and lining may shrink to different degrees. Use a professional cleaning service. Or you could use detachable linings. The curtains are made in much the same way, but with the use of a special double tape. The lining can then be removed, allowing both elements to be washed separately.

This lined curtain (LEFT) is part of a witty arrangement of wood cornice and gathered valance. Linings can be plain or patterned. Here, a traditional floral cotton is revealed when the curtains are folded back. Once they are closed, the unusual choice of lining fabric will be visible only to passersby. One note of caution, however: a mottled look may occur when a lining with a busy design is lit from behind by the sun.

MATERIALS
Face fabric
Lining
Weights
Stiffener (handmade headings)
Curtain tape (machine-stitched headings)

MEASURING
❑ Width: The flat, unpleated width should be two-and-a-half times the finished width. For the face fabric, add 3in (8cm) for side hems; for the lining, add 2in (5cm).
❑ Length: For the face fabric, add 6in (15cm) for the lower hem plus 3in (7.5cm) for the top hem; for the lining, add 4in (10cm) plus 1in (2.5cm).

MAKING UP
1. Cut out the widths of the face fabric and then the lining.
2. Join the fabric widths, and then join the lining widths.
3. Trim selvages and press open seams.
4. Turn up a double 2in (5cm) hem in the lining and stitch close to the fold.
5. Lay fabric face down. Make 1½in (4cm) side hems. Blind-catchstitch (see page 179) into position, ending 10in (25cm) from the base and from the top.
6. Sew the weights into lining bags (see page 91).
7. Turn up a double 3in (7.5cm) lower hem, miter the corners, and stitch the covered weights into the miters and at the base of vertical seams.
8. Slip stitch the hem.
9. If you are making the heading by hand,

insert the stiffener before the lining is attached to the back of the curtain. If you are using tape, stitch it on when the rest of the curtain is complete, after the lining has been attached.

Handmade heading
1. Cut the stiffener to the finished width of the curtain, and lay it on the back of the face fabric, the edges even with fabric's fold lines. If using fusible buckram, baste (*a*).

a

2. If using non-fusible buckram (*b*), blind-catchstitch all around. Turn back top and side edges of face fabric.

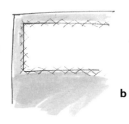

b

Locking in the lining
1. Lay the lining over the back of the curtain. The lower hem of the lining should lie 1in (2.5cm) above that of the finished curtain.
2. Turn under the side edge of the lining 1in (2.5cm) from the side edge of the curtain. Slip stitch along the fold, ending at the base of the stiffener. Then fold the lining back on itself,

forming a fold along the center of the lining. Lockstitch (see page 180) the length of the fold. Repeat along every seamline and half-width (*c* right). When you reach the other side, turn lining under; slip stitch 1in (2.5cm) from the edge.
3. If you are making a heading by hand, turn under the top of the lining 1in (2.5cm) from top edge; slip stitch (*d*).
4. If you are making a heading by hand using fusible buckram, remove the basting stitches and press with a hot iron to release the glue. Pleat or gather the heading (see pages 97, 99).

d

Machine-stitched heading
1. Make sure the top raw edges of the face fabric and lining are even, trimming if necessary.
2. Unless you are using a narrow tape, turn fabric and lining under by 1in (2.5cm) at the top, treating them as one layer. Position the tape on the back of the curtain just inside the top edge. Pin, baste, and stitch (see page 91) (*e* right).
3. If the heading is visible and you are using a narrow tape, turn the fabric and lining under by at least 2¾in (7cm) and place tape at least 2in (5cm) from the top edge.

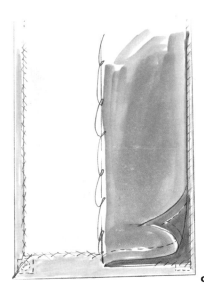

c

HANGING
Handmade heading
Attach pin-on or sew-on hooks to the back of the heading (see page 98).

Machine-stitched heading
1. If using corded tape, pull the cords in the tape at the outer edge until the curtain is the desired width, forming even pleats. Knot the cords and insert hooks along back of tape.

2. If using uncorded tape, insert pleater hooks in the pockets at regular intervals and pinch prongs together to form pleats.

TRAINING
To retain neat, uniform folds – particularly in the case of pinch-pleated headings – the curtain should be left tied up with strips of lining fabric for several days after hanging (see page 177).

e

Interlined Curtains

MATERIALS
Face fabric
Interlining
Lining
Weights
Stiffener (handmade heading)
Curtain tape (machine-stitched heading)

Making interlined curtains involves sandwiching a layer of interlining fabric between the face fabric and lining. A well made pair of interlined curtains will reward you by lasting for many years, their plump pleats giving a professional finish to any room. Furthermore, they will keep out the cold in winter and the heat in summer.

Interlined curtains, particularly when made up in a plain color, can take a variety of decorative features: a generous band of contrasting edging, lush fringes, or a padded edge. Visible headings are greatly enhanced with a looped line of cording, finished with knots and tassels – an effective way of making even inexpensive fabrics look special.

There are various interlining materials. Bump (a soft, thick, blanketlike cotton) and domette (a lighter version of bump) are the traditional fabrics, but these are imported and are only available from some custom drapery stores. Table felt or reinforced felt can sometimes be used instead of bump, and flannelette instead of domette. Synthetic interlining and needle-punched fleece are also available.

Making interlined curtains is a much easier task if you have the correct tools and a proper worktable. Of all the projects in this book, this one makes maximum use of the table: corners can be kept square and the time-consuming process of joining the interlining and lining is made relatively easy.

Do not forget that if a cornice or valance is to accompany the curtains, it should be made with the same lining and interlining (swags being an exception). A predominantly white fabric should have a bleached interlining and white lining; otherwise use an unbleached interlining and cream lining. Light will penetrate even interlined curtains (unless a blackout lining is used), so be careful not to mar the color of the fabric by using an inappropriately colored lining.

Points to remember

❑ Make sure that the layers of fabric, interlining, and lining lie flat, without wrinkles. Use clamps or covered bricks to hold everything neatly in place.

❑ Buy lining and interlining in the same width as the fabric so that seams align.

❑ Mark notches to identify the top and bottom of each length.

❑ Keep to the straight grain on plain fabrics; otherwise follow the pattern if possible.

❑ Unusually long pieces of thread are needed for locking stitches: avoid knotting the thread in the middle of a seam since this causes tension.

❑ Clip seams or trim selvages to prevent any pulling.

❑ Try not to lose pins inside the curtain – use glass-headed pins so they are easy to see.

MEASURING

❑ Width: The flat, unpleated width should be two-and-a-half times the finished width. For the face fabric and interlining add 4in (10cm) for the side hems; for the lining, add 3in (8cm).

❑ Length: For the face fabric, add 4in (10cm) for the lower hem plus 2in (5cm) for the top hem; for the interlining, add 4in (10cm) for the lower hem; for the lining, add 4in (10cm) plus 1in (2.5cm).

MAKING UP

1. Cut the widths of fabric, lining, and interlining, allowing for any pattern repeat.

2. Join the fabric widths and join the lining widths. Press open seams, trimming selvages to prevent pulling.

3. Overlap the widths of interlining by 1in (2.5cm) and join with a blind-catchstitch.

4. Make a double 2in (5cm) lower hem in the lining and stitch close to the fold.

Locking in the interlining

1. Place the face fabric face down. Line up the side and base edges with the edges of the table.

2. Lay the interlining on top, smoothing out any wrinkles. Clamp or hold in position with a heavy book.

3. Fold the interlining in half to form a fold along the center. Lockstitch from the finished top edge to the finished bottom edge, moving the fabric and interlining together up the table if necessary to finish the line of stitching (a).

4. Working out from the center of the curtain, continue to fold the interlining back on itself every half-width, working parallel lines of locking stitches along every seamline and half-width until you reach the side of the curtain. The final row of locking stitches should run along the foldline that will become the finished

side edge, holding the interlining into the side hem.

5. When the lines of locking stitches run from the leading edge to the outer edge, fold back the hem and lockstitch along the horizontal fold. Be sure to smooth the layers flat every time the curtain is moved on the table (b).

6. Flap over the side hems and blind-catchstitch into position, picking up only the interlining, not penetrating the front of the curtain, and finishing 10in (25cm) from top and base.

7. Turn up a 4in (10cm) lower hem.

8. Sew the weights into small lining fabric bags (see page 91).

9. Miter the lower corners, folding the interlining and fabric as one layer. Stitch the covered weights into the miters and also at the base of each vertical seamline.

10. Leaving the edge raw, blind-catchstitch the hem into position.

11. Like lined curtains, interlined curtains can have either handmade or machine-stitched headings. If you are making the heading by hand, insert the stiffener at this point, before the lining is attached to the curtain. If you are using tape, stitch it on after the lining has been attached.

Handmade heading

1. Cut the stiffener to the finished width of the curtain and lay it on the back of the curtain, with the edge against the foldlines.

2. If using fusible buckram, baste into place (c).

3. If using non-fusible buckram, blind-catchstitch the buckram into position around all four sides (d above).

4. Miter top corners.

Locking in the lining

1. Place the lining on the back of the curtain. The lower hem of the lining should lie 1in (2.5cm) above the base edge of the curtain.

2. In much the same way as the interlining was attached to the face fabric, lockstitch the lining to the interlining and again at every half-width (e below).

3. Turn under the sides of the lining 1in (2.5cm) from the edges along the top and sides. Slip stitch in place, extending

stitching 4in (10cm) around the base line (f above right).

4. If you are making a heading by hand using fusible buckram, first remove the basting stitches and then press with a hot iron to release the glue. Either pleat or gather the heading (see pages 97, 99).

Machine-stitched heading

Pin, baste, and stitch the curtain tape to the back of the heading (see page 91).

HANGING
Handmade heading

Attach pin-on or sew-on hooks to the back of the heading (see page 98).

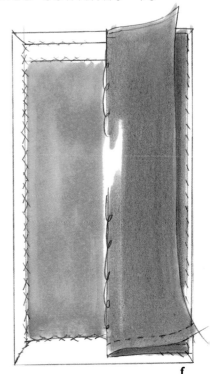

Machine-stitched heading

1. If using corded tape, pull until the curtain is the desired width, forming even pleats. Knot the cords and insert the hooks along the back of the tape.

2. If using uncorded tape, insert pleater hooks, pinching the prongs together to form pleats.

3. Bearing the weight of the curtain on your shoulder, insert the hooks directly into the rod or pole rings. Start from the center of the curtain and work outward – in this way, the weight of the curtain is distributed.

TRAINING

It is essential to train interlined curtains, particularly if they are pinch-pleated. Leave the curtains tied up with strips of lining fabric for at least a week after hanging (see page 177).

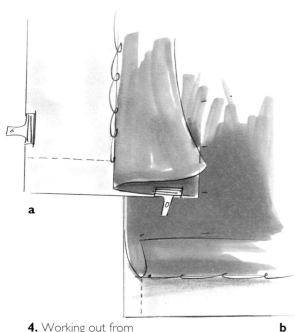

a

b

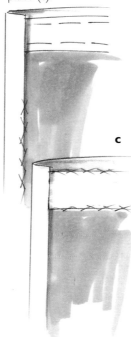

c

d

Headings
Handmade Headings

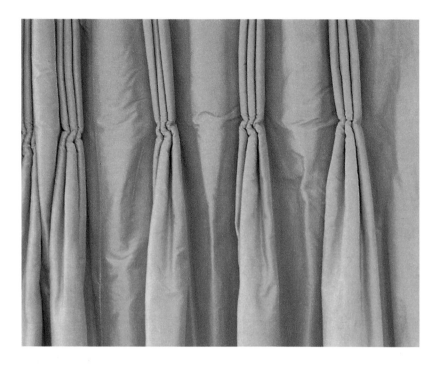

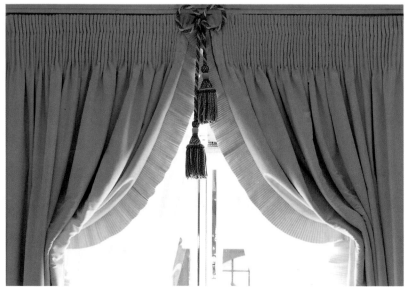

Classic pinch pleats are shown to effect in an apricot silk curtain (TOP), its heading free of any extraneous detail. A deep heading of handmade pencil pleats (ABOVE) is decorated with striped cord and tassels.

If a heading is to be hidden behind a cornice or valance, a sew-on heading is perfectly acceptable, but if it is visible, a handmade heading is preferable. Until fairly recently, handmade headings have been considered the province of the professional curtainmaker, and very little information was available to the amateur. Now, however, things are changing: a much wider range of materials can be obtained, and the techniques needed for handmade headings are much more accessible.

Many people cannot tell the difference between a machine-stitched or handmade heading, hardly noticing the telltale double line of machine stitching that attaches the curtain tape to the rest of the curtain. As the subtleties of curtainmaking become more apparent, however, so will the attractions of a handmade heading. A heading such as this requires little more effort than the machine-stitched equivalent, but gives greater flexibility of hook position and dispenses with untidy cords. To the connoisseur, a handmade heading is an essential part of truly professional-looking curtains.

The base of a handmade heading is a band of stiffener inserted behind the lining. This is sometimes crinoline but more often buckram, which is a heavily stiffened cotton. "Fusible" buckrams are impregnated with a glue that is released when the heading is pressed with a hot iron, thereby fusing them in position. "Non-fusible" buckram has to be blind-catchstitched into place, but is more easily dry cleaned. Once the buckram is in place, the heading is pleated by hand and sewn into position.

Pinch Pleats

Pinch pleats are the most commonly used headings. The curtain falls into folds that can be easily dressed and tied back, while the triple pleats are perfect for decorative cords. They can vary in depth.

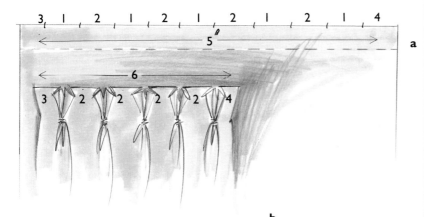

MEASURING

❑ Width: The flat unpleated width should be two-and-a-half times the finished width (a & b above).
❑ Decide on the length of the return (3) and the overlap (4), usually 3in (7.5cm). The flat areas between the pleats (2) plus the return (3) and the overlap (4) will add up to the finished width of the curtain (6). Each flat area (2) should measure about 6in (15cm).
❑ First subtract (3) and (4) from your finished width (6). Work out how many times (2) will fit into what is left.
❑ You now know how many spaces there will be between the pleats (2); add one for the number of pleats (1). Subtract the finished width (6) from the unfinished width (5) for what will be used up by pleating. Divide by the number of pleats to arrive at your (1) measurement.

❑ For example, if the finished width of the curtain is 45in (1.1m), the return (3) is 5in (12cm), and the overlap (4) is 3in (8cm), there will be 36in (90cm) left for the flat areas between the pleats (2). This will make six flat areas (2) and seven pleats (1). Since the unfinished heading (5) should be two-and-a-half times wider than the finished, pleated-up heading (6), (5) will be 45in (1.1m) × 2.5 = 112½ (2.75m). From this, subtract (6 × 2) + 3 + 4 = 6 = 45in (1.1m) and you are left with 67½in (1.65m). Divide this by the seven pleats and you are left with a (1) measurement of just over 9½in (23.5cm).

MAKING UP
1. Using pins, mark out the heading.
2. Make the pleats and stitch down the back of each one. The baseline of each pleat should be about ½in (12mm) above the baseline of the buckram (c).

3. Form each pleat into three sections, pressing the buckram into sharp edges (d).

4. Hand- or machine stitch across the base of the pleats (e & f).

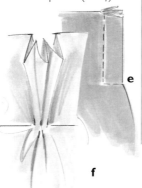

French Pleats

Sometimes known as goblet pleats, French pleats are closely related to pinch pleats and have much the same uses. They seem to work outstandingly well in combination with a curved valance shelf and stationary curtains (ABOVE). Like a pinch-pleat heading, this heading lends itself to the use of cording in figure eights and other knots, swagged loops, and tassels. A covered button sewn to the base of each pleat can make a very attractive finishing touch.

MAKING UP
1. Form the triple pleat at the base, sew into place, and push out the upper section into a cup shape.
2. Stuff the cup with a piece of batting or interlining (g).

Pencil Pleats

Handmade pencil pleats are something of a luxury, since curtain tape will do the job quite adequately. Like all handmade headings, however, they give a rich and professional finish to a pair of curtains, and will not create a double line of machine-stitching marring the front of the heading. Another advantage in making your own is the freedom to choose the precise depth of heading you want. Sew-on hooks, the alternative to pin-on hooks, are also usually the province of professional workrooms, but there is no reason why they should not be used by the amateur. All that is needed is accurate measuring – unlike pin-on hooks, it is difficult to vary the hook positions.

MEASURING
❑ Width: The flat, unpleated width should be two-and-a-half times finished width.

MAKING UP
1. Hand sew a double line of matched gathering stitches along the stiffened heading using strong thread. Leave one end loose. If a curtain is made from more than one width, use fresh thread for every width (h).

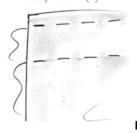

h

2. Gather up to the finished width.
3. Cut heading web (a cotton twill tape) to run along the back of the gathered heading. Cut a piece of lining to the same length, but double the width. Sew the lining to the back of the web (i).

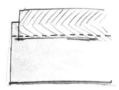

i

4. Sew the web to the back of the heading. It should run ¼–½ in (6–12mm) below the top of the curtain. Use a double row of backstitches, picking up the heading buckram each time.
5. Sew the hooks to the web, sewing through all the layers and forming small stitches that will be hidden in the back of the folds (j & k).

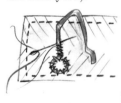

j

k

6. Turn the strip of lining over so that it covers the web, leaving the front of the hooks showing (l).

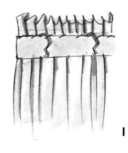

l

7. Slip stitch along the top and sides of the lining strip.

Smocked Heading

A smocked heading, such as the one shown above, can look most impressive. To sew such a heading is time-consuming but requires no special skill. Based on a pencil-pleated heading, the pleats are alternately linked, using small hand stitches, to form the lattice-work surface. Considerable padding is necessary for the smocked effect to look its best, so interlining is recommended. Smocked headings are suitable for use only with stationary curtains, which never need to be drawn back, as the smocking prevents the curtains from pulling back in a uniform manner. The overlap of stationary curtains is an ideal position for a decorative bow, rosette, or Maltese cross.

MAKING UP
1. A smocked heading can vary in width and scale according to the dimensions of the curtain.
2. Proceed as for pencil pleats (see left). When the pleats are made, mark alternating stitching points and sew the pleats together with small hand stitches (m).

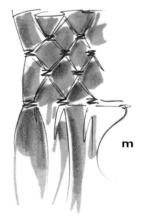

m

Gathered Heading

A narrow gathered heading gives a charming finish to small, dainty curtains. Avoid using buckram, since it is often too stiff for this type of heading. If a little extra padding is needed, fold a strip of interlining into the heading before it is gathered.

MEASURING
❑ Width: The flat, ungathered width should be two-and-half-times the finished curtain width.

MAKING UP
1. Run a double line of matching stitches along the heading and gather up in a similar way to pencil pleats (n & o).
2. Secure the pleats with a strip of heading web (strong cotton twill tape) sewn to the back of the heading. You can then attach pin-on or sew-on hooks. To save time, you can use a two-cord gathering tape – the result will be much the same.

n

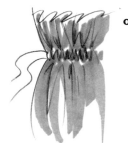

o

Poufed Heading

When the self-ruffle on a rod-pocket or gathered heading is fluffed out, it becomes a "poufed" heading. Instead of standing up from the pole in a stiff frill, a fat ruffle is formed along the heading. Little expertise is needed for this heading – the ruffle is merely pulled into shape and the two layers of fabric are separated a little. A layer of interlining, folded into the heading, creates a more solid effect.

MAKING UP
❑ Make up as for a rod-pocket heading, or gathered heading, leaving a generous self-frill along the top. The frill is then poufed out to form the fat ruffle that gives this heading its name (q).

q

Rod-Pocket Heading

A simple rod-pocket heading is used with light curtains or voiles. A more sophisticated version is described in detail in the project on page 104.

MEASURING
❑ Width: The flat, ungathered width should be two-and-a-half times the finished curtain width.

MAKING UP
1. Turn in the top edge twice and stitch close to the fold to form a casing.
2. Gather the curtain onto a dowel and mount at the window using rod sockets (p).

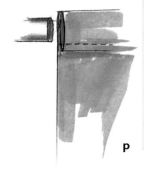

p

Unpleated Heading

Unpleated headings should be used only when the top of the curtain is visible and hanging from a decorative pole and rings, in which case the gently waved surface and lack of fussy heading shapes are welcome. This type of heading sometimes utilizes fabric ties or tabs that attach the curtain either to the rings or directly to the pole. Scallops are another popular heading for use with rings, especially for café curtains, and the no-sew curtain on page 136 has yet another type.

MEASURING
❑ Width: A curtain with an unpleated heading is only one-and-a-half, not the usual two-and-a-half, times wider than the window space that it is to occupy.

MAKING UP
1. Insert the stiffener behind the lining in the usual way, but do not pleat or gather the heading.
2. Sew ties to the back of the heading (see page 101) and tie in bows or knots to the curtain rings or directly onto the pole (r).

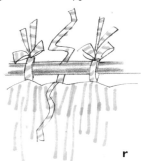

r

Corded Heading

Decorative cording gives an elegant finish to grand draperies. The cord is stitched at the base of the pleats and the loops are left to find their own lines. There are many different ways of looping and tying cord and tassels, but care should be taken not to overload a heading; simplicity is often the key to success.

MAKING UP

1. Pin the cord to the front of the heading. Using a long, fine needle, sew it on to the heading with strong thread. The needle picks up a few threads from the front of the drapes and the back of the cord with each stitch (s).

s

2. Never try to attach a cord once the drapes are hung – working on a ladder for long periods with your arms held high is exhausting.

PROJECT
Curtain with Tied Heading

Tied or tab headings are certainly one of the simplest ways to hang curtains. The headings may be knotted to wood or brass curtain rings, or looped over the pole itself. Tied to rings, the curtains will slide back smoothly. Fabric ties, however, tend to stick when drawn over a pole, and therefore may be more suitable if the curtains are not intended to be opened and closed regularly. Headings cannot easily be tied to metal or plastic rods, which need curtain hooks to operate effectively.

Tied headings give an informal look and work well for light kitchen or bathroom curtains, although they sometimes also suit the stiffened headings of heavy lined curtains. By varying the shape and size of the ties, from narrow ribbons to fat bows, you can change the effect from tailored to the voluptuous.

To avoid fussiness, ties are often best with plainer curtains. Well-stiffened headings are less likely to droop between the ties. Otherwise, place the ties at frequent intervals.

For this cheerful kitchen curtain, a piece of checked fabric has been lined with striped material and tied to a simple wooden dowel. By day the curtain is caught with a bow to reveal the rooftop view. It is easy to remove for cleaning, and the absence of stiffening in the heading reduces the risk of shrinkage.

MATERIALS
Face fabric
Lining

FITTINGS
Dowel
Rod sockets

TOOLS
Drill or awl

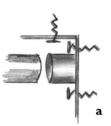

a

FITTING
Attach dowel to the top of the window using top- or face-fixing rod sockets (*a & b*).

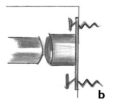

b

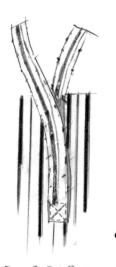

6. To make ties, fold strips in half lengthwise, right sides together, and stitch around two sides. Trim corners, turn, and press. Tuck in the open ends and stitch across.

7. Fold all but one of the ties in half. Pin them to the back at intervals 4in (10cm) from the top edge. Stitch in place (d & e).

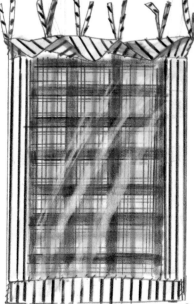

HANGING
Tie the finished curtain to the dowel. Tie one strip around the center of the curtain.

MAKING UP

1. Cut the face fabric to the length of the window, adding 12in (30cm) to the width to allow the curtain to drape slightly between the ties.

2. Cut the lining, allowing an extra 6in (15cm) all around.

3. Cut the desired number of heading ties in the form of fabric strips 36 × 6in (90 × 15cm).

4. Pin the face fabric to the lining, right sides together, down the side edges, leaving 6in (15cm) of lining showing top and bottom. Stitch, turn, and press. Equal bands of lining will show on either side (c right).

5. Turn the lower and upper edges of the lining over to the front of the curtain, then tuck in, pin, and slip stitch in place.

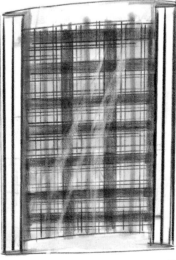

PROJECT
Tab Heading

One of the most straightforward ways of slotting a curtain onto a pole is by means of a tab heading. No knots, bows, hooks, or rings are necessary. Instead, simple strips of fabric fold over the pole and are attached to the back of a pleated or unpleated, stiffened, or unstiffened, heading.

This tab heading runs along an unlined curtain whose top edge has merely been given a double ¾in (19mm) hem. The loops are secured with a double line of stitches. Thanks to the lightness of the curtain, the closely spaced tabs, and the lack of any extra fullness, the heading does not drape between the loops.

MAKING UP
1. Measure the circumference of the curtain pole allowing extra length for the ties to be sewn to the back of the heading. The width of the ties should be twice the finished width plus two seam allowances. Cut out the required number of ties.
2. Fold the strips in half lengthwise, right sides together.
3. Pin and stitch along the side and also along one end.

4. Turn, trim the corners, and press. Fold into loops.
5. Pin the tabs at regular intervals along the back of the heading. Stitch into place with two lines of stitching (a).

a

HANGING
Slot the pole through the tabs.

PROJECT
Cable Top

These stenciled curtains use heading web (strong cotton twill tape) to stiffen their headings. Metal eyelets are then threaded with lengths of cord which tie the curtain to the pole. This striking treatment is suitable for unlined curtains scarcely wider than the window.

MAKING UP
1. Pin a length of 2in (5cm) heading web to the top of the curtain and attach with two lines of stitching.
2. Using a special eyelet tool insert a line of eyelets at regular intervals along the length of the web.

3. Measure out cord to slot through the eyelets and around the pole. Cut into lengths. Thread each length of cord through an eyelet, and knot.

HANGING
Run the pole through the loops of cord and fix into place (a).

a

VARIATION
Swedish Bow

Bows set against a sheer muslin curtain make for a simple but graceful scheme. The curtains have been given wide, pencil-pleated headings (see page 98) behind which lengths of narrow ribbon have been sewn on. The lightness of the curtain fabric means that even delicate ribbon can be used (*a*).

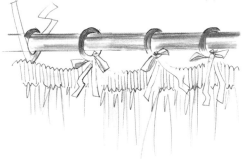

a

VARIATION
Zigzag Top

Shaped tops such as these zigzags are easy to make and lend an amusing air to a small cotton curtain.

MAKING UP
1. Cut face fabric and lining, adding 4in (10cm) to the length of the face fabric and 3in (7.5cm) to the lining. Add 1in (2.5cm) to the width.
2. Using a pattern, cut a zigzag edge along the top of both.
3. Place fabric and lining right sides together. Pin, baste, and stitch around the zigzags and three-quarters of the side seams (*a*).

4. Turn and press.
5. Make double 2in (5cm) lower hems in the fabric and lining. Blind-catchstitch the hem of the face fabric; stitch the lining hem. Finish the side seams with slip stitches.
6. Insert eyelets with an eyelet tool.

HANGING
Use split brass rings to hang the curtain from the brass pole (*b*).

a

b

A plain stiffened heading is pierced with eyelets and slotted along a rod (ABOVE).

PROJECT
Plaid Bordered Rod-Pocket Curtain

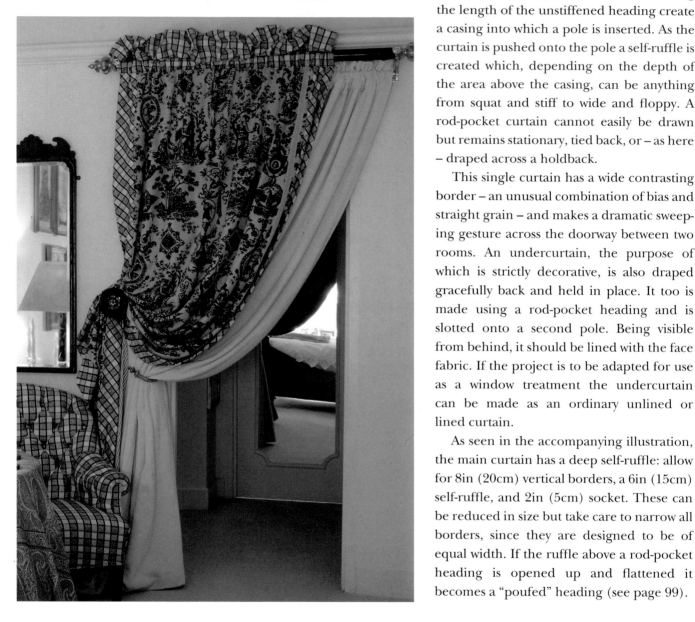

A rod-pocket heading is one of the simplest headings. Two lines of stitching the length of the unstiffened heading create a casing into which a pole is inserted. As the curtain is pushed onto the pole a self-ruffle is created which, depending on the depth of the area above the casing, can be anything from squat and stiff to wide and floppy. A rod-pocket curtain cannot easily be drawn but remains stationary, tied back, or – as here – draped across a holdback.

This single curtain has a wide contrasting border – an unusual combination of bias and straight grain – and makes a dramatic sweeping gesture across the doorway between two rooms. An undercurtain, the purpose of which is strictly decorative, is also draped gracefully back and held in place. It too is made using a rod-pocket heading and is slotted onto a second pole. Being visible from behind, it should be lined with the face fabric. If the project is to be adapted for use as a window treatment the undercurtain can be made as an ordinary unlined or lined curtain.

As seen in the accompanying illustration, the main curtain has a deep self-ruffle: allow for 8in (20cm) vertical borders, a 6in (15cm) self-ruffle, and 2in (5cm) socket. These can be reduced in size but take care to narrow all borders, since they are designed to be of equal width. If the ruffle above a rod-pocket heading is opened up and flattened it becomes a "poufed" heading (see page 99).

MATERIALS
Face fabric
Interlining
Lining
Contrasting fabric
Braid

FITTINGS
Pole
Brackets
Tieback

MEASURING
❑ Width: The flat width should be twice the finished width.
❑ Allow an extra 8in (20cm) plus one seam allowance for the top ruffle frill, 4in (10cm) for the lower hem.
❑ Contrasting fabric: Allow for an 11in (28cm) bias strip twice the finished length of the curtain plus hem allowances. Allow for a 9in (23cm) deep top border cut on the straight grain.

FITTING
Mount a pole above the doorway using brackets (see page 171). It should extend beyond the doorway by 12in (30cm) on each side, not including finials. The brackets should be flush with the edges of the finials.

MAKING UP
1. Cut the required number of widths in face fabric, lining, and interlining.
2. Cut an 11in (28cm) bias strip of contrasting fabric to run along the outer and leading edges.
3. Cut a 9in (23cm) strip of contrasting fabric on the straight grain for the top curtain border.

4. Join the widths of face fabric and attach the side borders (see page 182). Then press open seams.

5. If seams are needed along the top border, use flat-fell seams.

6. Make up as for an ordinary interlined curtain (see page 94), but leave the top edge raw and unstiffened. At this stage the curtain is the finished length plus one seam allowance.

7. Make double ½in (12mm) hems in the side edges of the remaining contrasting border (straight grain). Stitch into place close to the fold.

8. Place the right side of the contrasting border against the wrong side of the curtain top. Pin, baste, and stitch them together (*a*).

a

9. Turn the border over the top of the curtain. Turn under the lower edge of the border and slip stitch into place.

10. Mark parallel lines above and below the casing for the pole. A 2in (5cm) space between the lines of stitching is usually enough. The lower line

should be positioned just above the lower edge of the contrasting border. Baste and stitch the two lines, leaving the ends open. The casing should be neither too loose nor

b

too tight so the pole fits in snugly (*b*).

11. Slip stitch two short lines to close up the open ends of the ruffle.

12. Pin and hand sew the braid to the curtain.

13. Gather the curtain onto the pole.

14. Drape the curtain over the holdback.

VARIATION
Silk Curtains

This pair of rod-pocket curtains is more typical of the style than the single curtain in the main project. The heading is made using the face fabric, giving the impression of being simply folded over the front of the curtains. The self-ruffle formed above the casing is complemented by a disciplined self-ruffle along the leading edges.

A gilded surface is always best seen against a rich color and fabric. Here the dulled gold of the holdbacks is set off most effectively against the folds of deep green silk.

MAKING UP
Make up as for the single curtain in the main project, taking note of these points:

1. The pole has no finials. Accommodate the brackets between the front of the casing and the pole (see page 173) via the holes in the back of the casing. Close the open ends of the casing with a line of slip stitches, and baste to the end surface of the pole using finishing nails (*a*).

a

2. Since the curtains cover the whole length of the pole instead of two-thirds, make the flat width of each curtain two-and-a-half times the finished curtain width.

3. Instead of a contrasting top border, allow for a band of the same fabric. Reduce the dimensions to allow for a narrower ruffle. The band should measure the depth of the ruffle plus an allowance for the casing plus two seam allowances.

4. Position the holdbacks well inside the outer edges of the curtains.

5. A ruffle (see page 183) decorates the leading edges.

PROJECT
Muslin Curtain with Fan-Pleated Heading

Made in sheer muslin and with a contrasting band, this fan-pleated scalloped heading is unusual and charming. It is well adapted to the lightweight fabric: a heavier cloth would not pleat up so effectively.

MATERIALS
Face fabric
Lining
Contrasting fabric
6in (15cm) deep stiffener such as crinoline
Pin-on hooks

MEASURING
❑ Width: The flat unpleated width should be two-and-a-half times finished width.

MAKING UP
1. Calculate the dimensions of the heading (see page 97). Make a pattern of the heading shape. The curves (*1*) will be pleated; the loops (*2*) will link them.
2. Cut out the face fabric, leaving ½in (12mm) for top hem.
3. Cut out the same in a strip of white lining fabric, 6in (15cm) deep. Turn under a small amount along the base of the lining and stitch close to the fold.
4. Lay the stiffener on back of heading.
5. If using non-fusible stiffener, pin and blind-catchstitch the base of the stiffener to the fabric (*a*). Otherwise, baste into place.

6. Turn the top of the fabric over it, clipping where necessary. Baste close to the edge.
7. Lay the lining strip over the back of the heading. Pin and turn in the top edge, clipping where necessary. Baste.
8. Turn in the side and lower hems and stitch (see page 181).
9. Cut a bias strip in the contrasting fabric and attach (see page 182).
10. Pleat up the scalloped sections into five small pleats, stitching the base of each (*b & c*).

b

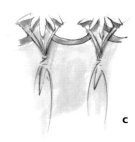

c

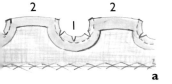

a

HANGING
Pierce the back of the pleats with pin-on hooks. Hang in the usual way.

Curtain Tapes

Sewn-in tapes stiffen curtain headings, contain pockets into which hooks are slotted, and are stitched to the backs of curtain headings. Sometimes parallel lines of cords run through the tape; once the curtain is made, these cords are pulled to form the requisite heading shapes. Other tapes utilize pleater hooks with prongs that create the pinch pleats. Available in a range of widths, tapes vary in quality and detail.

GATHERED
A two-cord gathering tape is suitable for a light curtain or valance. With a hidden heading, the tape runs along the top edge; with an exposed heading, when a ruffle is appropriate, the tape is set down by at least 2in (5cm) (*a*).

PENCIL PLEATS
This tape is the ideal choice for formal pencil pleats. It is suitable for lined or interlined curtains and valances (*b*).

PINCH PLEATS
This tape – either corded, or uncorded and used with pleater hooks – will form triple pleats, which can then be secured by hand sewing if desired. Use it for lined or interlined curtains and valances (*c*).

SMOCKED
Smocking tape does not create the latticework effect of hand smocking (see page 98) but a distinctive effect a little like gathering.

SHEER
This open-mesh tape is less opaque than other tapes and will complement sheer or lace fabrics.

DETACHABLE LINING
A special tape is used when a detachable lining is required.

HOOK-AND-LOOP
This tape does not need hooks, but is drawn up to form a rear surface suitable for attaching to hook-and-loop tape, eliminating the need to stitch lines of hook-and-loop tape to the backs of balloon shades, or valances.

HOOKS
Plastic hooks are best for holding sheer, unlined, or simple lined curtains, but brass hooks are preferable for heavier, interlined curtains. A woven slot, available on some tapes, will hold each hook firmly in place and avoid sagging. A 1in (2.5cm) tape has only one hook pocket while wider tapes have two or three, allowing the length of the curtains to be varied. The bottom row is used if the rod is to be covered when the curtains are closed, and the top row is used if it is to be exposed. An uncorded tape uses pronged pleater hooks, which slot into vertical pockets and are then pinched together to form pinch pleats (*d*).

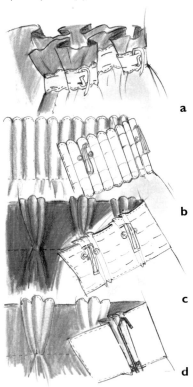

a

b

c

d

Valances

MATERIALS
Face fabric
Lining
Stiffener
Hook-and-loop tape
Cord
Fringe
Stiff brown paper or
newspaper (pattern)

FITTINGS
Valance shelf
Brackets
Curtain rod
Tieback hooks

TOOLS
Drill
Awl
Staple gun or hammer
and tacks

FITTING
1. Prepare the valance shelf (see page 175).
2. Staple or tack a line of hook-and-loop tape to the front edges and returns.
3. Attach the curtain rod to the valance shelf, and the shelf to the wall.
4. Fix the tieback hooks to the wall in position.

Avalance is like a miniature curtain, hung over the top of the window from a valance shelf. Valances can take many forms, from a simple band of lace, unsupported by curtains of any sort, to an elaborate arrangement of gathering and pleating, made to accompany a pair of heavy curtains or drapes below. Whereas cornices and lambrequins have a flat surface, pulled over a stiff backing, a valance is soft, either draped, gathered, or folded, and can be lined and interlined. Its purpose is partly decorative, partly practical. Visually, a valance will help to balance the curtains below. Decoratively, it can make a considerable contribution – the permutations of cording, swagging, pleating, and trimming are almost endless. On a practical note, it hides the curtain rod.

The lower edge of a valance can be treated in numerous ways – cut into a serpentine shape or edged with a contrasting band, fringe, or fan-edging. The upper edge, too, can be put to use – a looped cord or line of rosettes are just two of the many possibilities.

The valance should be in proportion to the window, never shallow or too short, yet should not blot out too much light. If this is the case, consider either raising the valance shelf slightly so that the valance covers some of the wall above the window, or use an attached valance that can be pulled back with the curtains.

Like so many other treatments, one basic shape, made up in different fabrics and with a variety of trimmings, can be used in any number of settings.

PROJECT

Bell-Pleated Damask Valance

In this project the valance, made up in sections and edged in silky fringe, was taken from an 1840 upholsterer's manual. The delicate cream damask and gently tapering bells lend tranquil symmetry to a living room.

The valance and curtains are backed in plain lining fabric and decorated with fringe and cord to match the tassel tiebacks. The curtains themselves have been lightly gathered, the flat width being only one-and-a-half times the finished width, while the valance shelves have been decorated with a discreet bow on the front edges, lending a subtle rhythm to the line of windows.

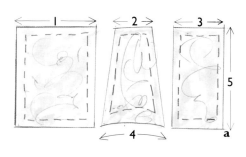

MAKING UP
1. The valance is made from alternating pieces of fabric, tapered to form the bells and rectangular to form the linking panels. Longer side panels take the valance fabric around the returns of the shelf.

2. By figuring out how many flat sections (between bells) will fit along the front assess how many bells there will be (see pinch pleats, page 97).
3. Experiment with paper cut-outs to find the correct proportions for the window in

question. Make patterns (see page 115) that include a seam allowance.
4. Cut out the two side panels, the bells, and the rectangular panels in face fabric and lining. Each should show the same part of any pattern (*a* left).

5. Join the alternating pieces, first in the face fabric, then the lining. Press open seams (b).
6. Cut out pieces of stiffener 3in (7.5cm) deep, to strengthen the valance heading. If using fusible buckram, each piece will fit under the seam allowance 1½in (3.8cm) below the top edge of the heading (b).

7. Baste into position. Blind-catchstitch around each section (non-fusible buckram).
8. Place the lining and face fabric right sides together. Pin and stitch along the base, leaving 1½in (3.8cm) free at each end for hems. Turn and press the lower edge.
9. Turn the lining in around the other three sides, and slip stitch.

10. Remove basting from one panel at a time and press with a hot iron to release glue (fusible buckram).

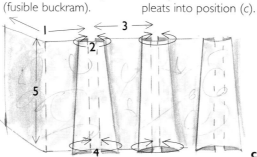

c

11. Pleat the valance by bringing the vertical seams together behind each pleat, and baste pleats into position (c).

12. Attach the fringe to the lower edge.
13. Pin the cord along the front and hand sew into position (d).

14. Pin and hand sew the hook-and-loop tape to the back of the heading 1½in (3.8cm) below top edge (e).

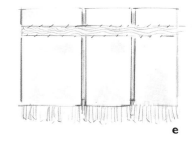

e

HANGING
Join the lines of hook-and-loop tape.

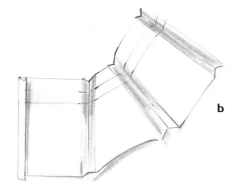

b

d

VARIATION
Gathered Bell-Pleated Valance

This feminine concoction of bell pleats and miniature swags has its main part cut out in one continuous strip, which is then gathered and pleated onto a band of covered buckram. The valance dips down a little at either end, framing the window in an attractive repeated loop. If you wish to make the valance appear more substantial, use a light interlining and treat it as a single layer with the face fabric.

Pale Roman shades pull down behind the curtains, offering an alternative means of covering the window and making for a most effective blackout system.

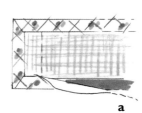
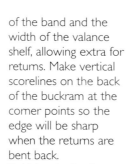

MATERIALS
Face fabric
Interlining (to cover stiffener)
Lining
Heavyweight buckram
Contrasting fabric
Piping cord
Hook-and-loop tape

FITTINGS
Valance shelf
Curtain rod
Roman shade batten and fittings

FITTING
1. Prepare a wood valance shelf to the desired width. Make sure it is deep enough for a curtain rod and Roman shade fittings.
2. Screw a 2 × 2in (5 × 5cm) wood batten to the back edge of the valance shelf. Fix a curtain rod in front of the shade fittings. Run screw eyes along the base of the shade batten. Staple hook-and-loop tape to the front edge of the shelf.
3. Fix the valance shelf to the wall using strong brackets since with the shades and the curtains, the shelf will take a lot of strain. If the shelf is hung well above the window recess, there may be room to have an independent Roman shade fitting directly above the window molding.

MAKING UP
1. Cut a strip of heavyweight buckram to the finished depth of the band and the width of the valance shelf, allowing extra for returns. Make vertical scorelines on the back of the buckram at the corner points so the edge will be sharp when the returns are bent back.
2. Using the buckram as a pattern, cut out the face fabric, interlining, and lining, allowing 1in (2.5cm) extra all around for the fabric, ¾in (19mm) for the interlining, and ½in (12mm) for the lining.
3. Lay the buckram over the interlining. Stretch the overlap of the interlining over the edge of the buckram. Trim the corners to remove bulk. If using non-fusible buckram, blind-catchstitch around all four sides. If using fusible buckram, press the seam allowance with a hot iron to release the glue in the buckram.
4. Lay the buckram strip on the face fabric,

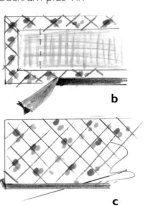

and turn under all four edges (a).
5. Blind-catchstitch the fabric to the interlining beneath (if using non-fusible buckram). Then press the edges with a hot iron so as to fuse the fabric and buckram (if using fusible buckram).
6. Cut a bias strip of contrasting fabric and prepare the welting (see page 182) to the length of the buckram plus 1in (2.5cm) for end seam allowances. Pin and slip stitch the welting to the base of the buckram strip (b & c).
7. Prepare a second bias strip for the

contrasting edging along the top of the band. Fold in half lengthwise; press. Turn under ½ in (12mm) and press. Place the fold of the bias strip along the top edge of the buckram band, with the turned-under edge to the front and the raw edge along the back. Pin and slip stitch along the front of the band. Baste the back of the edging to the fabric and interlining.

8. Prepare a pattern for the ruffle section of the valance (d).

9. The distances (3–5) and (4–6) are equal to the depth of the buckram strip and will be the side edges of the triple pleats – the (3–4) measurement will fold into the pleats themselves. The pleats appear to be part of the buckram bands but are actually sewn on separately. The (1–2) measurement is the distance between the bell pleats. The depth of the valance should be about one-fifth of the length of the curtains, dipping to slightly more at the sides. The curving lower edge gives the valance its lower edge of alternating loops.

10. The gathered effect between the bell sections is achieved by gathering (2–9) onto (5–9) and (1–10) onto (6–10); (2–9) and (6–10) should be one-and-a-half times the length of (5–9) or (6–10).

11. Cut out the pattern in face fabric and in lining. Pleat or gather (2–9) and (1–10) either by hand

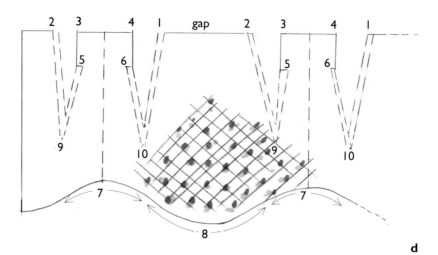

d

or using gathering stitches, and pin onto (5–9) and (6–10) respectively. Baste and stitch into position, ending ¾ in (19mm) from the end (where 2 meets 5 and 1 meets 6) (e below). Repeat the same process, this time in the lining fabric.

12. Lay the face fabric and lining with right sides together. Pin, baste, and stitch along the lower edge and sides. Press the seams, trim the corners, and turn. Baste around the top, ½ in (12mm) from the edge.

13. Cut the contrasting bias strip for the lower edge. Lay against the edge, pin, baste, and stitch. Fold the contrasting fabric over to the back and slip stitch into place (see page 180).

14. Turn in the lining and the face fabric around the triple-pleat section (5–3–4–6) and slip stitch around the three sides.

15. Prepare another bias strip in contrasting fabric and attach it to the top of the pleat section (3–4) as for the lower edge of the valance.

16. Form the pleated sections into triple pleats, then pin, and hand sew into place at the base.

17. Join the buckram band to the ruffle. The pleat sections lie along the surface of the band, and the top seam allowances of the swag sections are slotted behind the lower edge of the band. Pin, baste, and slip stitch the ruffle in place (f & g below).

18. Pin, baste, and stitch a line of hook-and-loop tape along the front of the buckram band lining ½ in (12mm) from the top edge. Lay the lining over the back of the buckram strip, turn in on all four sides, and slip stitch (h).

19. Prickstitch below the line of tape (non-fusible buckram). Press with a hot iron to release the glue (fusible buckram).

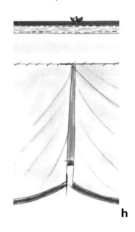

h

20. Remove all pins and visible basting stitches.

HANGING
Join the lines of hook-and-loop tape.

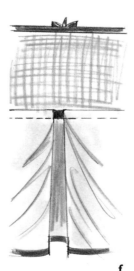

e

f

g

PROJECT
Box-Pleated Valance

A box-pleated ruffle brings a touch of formality to a soft valance. Made in a sprigged cotton, it is well adapted to this bedroom window; or, in a more sophisticated fabric, it can take on a much grander look, particularly with a coordinating fringe.

MATERIALS
Face fabric
Interlining
Lining
Heavyweight buckram
Welting cord
Contrasting fabric
Hook-and-loop tape

FITTINGS
Valance shelf
Brackets
Curtain rod

MEASURING
❑ Depth: The depth of the valance should be one-fifth of the curtain length. The pleated ruffle is twice the depth of the flat panel.

Panel
❑ Width: buckram: equal to the front and returns of the valance shelf plus 1in (2.5cm) for corners; fabric and lining: the same plus 2in (5cm) for seam allowances; interlining: the same plus 1in (2.5cm) for seam allowances.
❑ Depth: buckram: equal to the finished depth; fabric and lining: the same plus 2in (5cm) for seam allowances; interlining: the same plus 1in (2.5cm) for seam allowances.

Box-pleated ruffle
❑ Width: The flat width should be two-and-a-half times the finished width plus 2in (5cm) for seam allowances (fabric, lining, and interlining). For pleats that butt up, allow three times the width.
❑ Depth: Add 2in (5cm) to the finished depth for hem and seam allowance (fabric, lining, and interlining).

Piping cord and bias strip
❑ Length: Both are equal to the width of the shelf plus returns, plus two seam allowances.

FITTING
1. Fix the curtain rod to the base of the valance shelf.
2. Staple hook-and-loop tape to the front edge of the shelf.
3. Fix the valance shelf above the window using strong brackets.

MAKING UP
1. Cut out the buckram strip. Score to make bending the returns easier.
2. Cut and join the widths of fabric, interlining, and lining for the panel and ruffle. Position any pattern in the fabric carefully, using central and side panels if more than one width is used.
3. Prepare the welting (see page 182).

4. Lay the buckram over the fabric and interlining. Starting at the center and working outward, stretch first the interlining and then the fabric over the back of the buckram, and secure with blind-catchstitch (non-fusible buckram) or fuse the layers together by releasing the glue with the tip of a hot iron (fusible buckram). Trim any bulk at the corners (a).

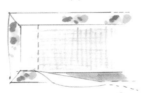

a

5. Pin and slip stitch the welting to the lower edge (b & c).

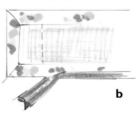

b

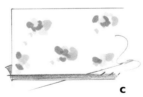

c

6. Prepare a bias strip in the contrasting fabric (see page 182). Fold in half lengthwise and press. Turn under one edge and press. Lay over the top edge of the buckram band. Slip stitch the folded edge to the front of the band. Baste the back to the fabric/interlining seam allowance.
7. Stitch the lining and fabric for the ruffle along the lower edge, right sides together.

Trim and press so that the fabric extends ½in (12mm) up the back of the lining.
8. Open out and lay the interlining so that its raw bottom edge fits into the base fold. Blind-catchstitch the interlining around all four sides (d).

d

9. Fold the lining back over, turn in the sides and slip stitch. Baste along the seamline (e).

e

10. Using pins, mark the center point of the ruffle.
11. Decide how many pleats there will be and where they will fall. If using a patterned fabric, try to repeat the same part of the design on the front of each box pleat. Mark out with pins dividing each

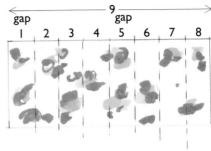

f

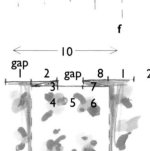

g

pleat and flat area into eight equal parts (1–8). Match the foldlines and pleat into half the flat width (9) to form (10) (f & g). Baste.
12. Starting from the center and marrying the center points of the panel and ruffle, pin the ruffle to the panel, picking up the seam allowances on the back of the buckram panel. Slip stitch in place below the welting (h & i).

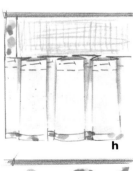

h

i

13. Pin, baste, and stitch a line of hook-and-loop tape 1in (2.5cm) below the top, raw edge of the lining.

14. Lay the lining over the back of the buckram panel, turn in, and slip stitch around all four sides (j).

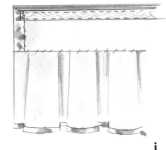

j

15. Press with a hot iron to release the glue and secure the lining (fusible buckram). Using long stitches to minimize visibility, prickstitch just below the line of the fastening to hold firmly in position (non-fusible buckram).

HANGING

Bend the valance at the corners and pinch to give a sharp edge. Mark the center of the shelf and the valance. Starting at the center and working outward, join the lines of hook-and-loop tape.

PROJECT
Serpentine Valance

A single basic technique may be used in scores of ways to create as many different effects as you like. A slight change of outline, trimming, or detail can create an entirely new look.

Here, a curved edge and gathered heading give the valance its particular features. The standard serpentine valance has a plain gathered heading and is often decorated with a line of fringe or contrasting binding along the lower and upper edges. In this example, white lining overlaps the edges to emphasize the curve and bring a welcome horizontal line to the busy vertical stripes. In addition to its interesting shape and contrasting trimming, this valance could have a fringe, cording, rosettes, or even bows.

Making a gathered valance requires much the same technique as making a lined or interlined curtain: the layers of fabric, interlining, and lining are assembled, and the heading is made up and pleated. There is one difference: unless the valance is particularly deep, you do not need to interlock the layers. If the draperies are interlined, the valance should be too.

MATERIALS
Face fabric
Lining
Interlining (optional)
Pencil-pleat tape or
  stiffener
Hook-and-loop tape
Stiff brown paper or
  newspaper (pattern)

FITTINGS
Valance shelf
Curtain rod
Brackets
Roman shade fittings
Tieback hooks

MEASURING
❑ Width: The flat, ungathered width should be two-and-a-half times the finished width.

❑ Depth: The side depth is one-fifth of the length of the drapery, narrowing to only one-eighth of the overall length at the center.

❑ Work out how many widths of fabric will be needed and multiply by the side depth, plus two seam allowances, to arrive at the total quantity.

FITTING
1. Prepare and fix the valance shelf, drapery and shade fittings, and tieback hooks.
2. Staple hook-and-loop tape to front and side edges of shelf.

MAKING UP

1. Cut out the widths of face fabric, lining, and interlining to the same length, i.e. the longest part of the valance plus two seam allowances.

2. Avoid a central seamline by using a central panel of face fabric, lining, and interlining, adding the rest of the fabric to each side.

3. Join the widths of face fabric. Then join the lining widths, and finally the interlining widths: either overlap the interlining and blind-catchstitch it, or turn it on its side to avoid the need for joins. Press.

4. Make a newspaper pattern of the flat valance. Fold the paper in half lengthwise and make a mark on the fold to show the narrowest part of the valance. With a fluid motion, carefully draw the curve from the center to the outer edge of the valance, using a felt pen or dotted pencil line (a below).

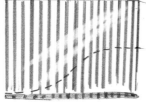

a

5. Cut along the line and open out.

6. Using the pattern, cut out the shape in interlining.

7. Blind-catchstitch the interlining pieces together (if necessary) and remove the pins.

8. Cut the same shape in the face fabric, allowing an extra 1in (2.5cm) along the top for the hem. Make sure that any fabric pattern falls correctly in the center.

9. Cut out the same in lining, allowing 1in (2.5cm) extra along the top and base for hems.

10. Lay down the fabric and lining, right sides together, lower edges flush with one another. Pin, baste, and stitch along the lower edge (b).

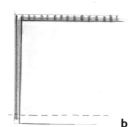

b

11. Turn and press the seam, with both parts over the fabric side of the seamline.

12. Clip to relieve any tension on the curve.

13. Place the wrong sides of the lining and fabric together and press so that the base of the lining overlaps the front of the valance by ½in (12mm).

14. If you do not wish a band of lining to show, make the seamline along the back of the valance, ½in (12mm) above the fold.

15. Lay the valance so it is fabric side down. Open out and use the ironed fold as a guide for the interlining.

16. Lay the interlining against the back of the fabric so that the base of the interlining runs along the foldline. Pin into place and run a line of blind catch stitches along the bottom edge.

17. Pick up only a few threads of fabric with each stitch. Remove the pins (c).

c

18. If a stiffener is being used, now is the time to insert it. It should lie 3½in (9cm) below the top edge.

19. Blind-catchstitch into place (if using non-fusible buckram) or baste (if using fusible buckram).

20. Fold the lining back over the interlining. Pin the layers together at intervals.

21. Turn under the fabric and interlining at the sides and top. Turn under the side edges and top of the lining and slip stitch around all three sides.

22. Press with a hot iron to release glue (if using fusible buckram).

23. Run two lines of matched stitches ½in (12mm) from the upper and lower edges of the stiffener, penetrating all layers.

24. If using pencil-pleat tape, place it over the back, 3in (7.5cm) from the top edge.

25. Pin, baste, and stitch, starting both lines of stitching from the same end to avoid puckering. Leave the cords in the tape free at each end (d).

26. Pull up the cords or thread to the

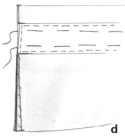

d

finished width of the valance, forming tighter gathers at 4in (10cm) intervals, creating the scalloped shape that runs along the top of the valance.

27. Slip stitch the hook and-loop tape to the back of the heading (e & f).

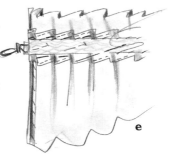

e

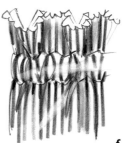

f

HANGING

1. Hang the valance after the shade and draperies. Make sure that there is plenty of room for the draperies and shade to operate efficiently without interfering with the back of the valance.

2. Join the lines of hook-and-loop tape on the valance and the valance shelf.

MATERIALS
Fabric
Pendants
Stiff brown paper or
  newspaper (pattern)

FITTINGS
Curtain pole
Brackets
Roller shade

PROJECT
Arched Valance

This elegantly arched valance lends an air of stately sophistication to a high window, but the actual sewing techniques themselves are not difficult. The valance needs no stiffening, hooks, or specialized equipment and hangs from a simple pole. However, like all projects that involve drapery, extra care is required to make sure that preliminary calculations are correct.

The valance softens the daylight that comes through the top of the window, its majestic appearance well suited to the surroundings. Heavy pendants pull the tips into shape but, if these are difficult to find, they could be replaced by improvised objects, perhaps tassels or decorative beads.

A roller shade in the same fabric pulls down at night to blank out the window.

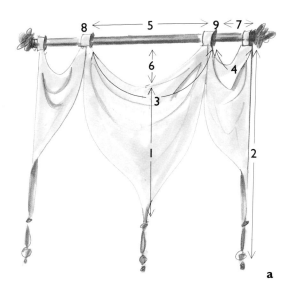

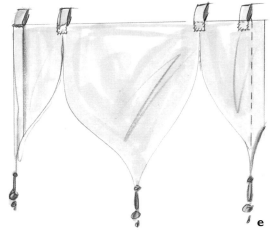

a

MEASURING

(a above)

1. The valance is lined with the face fabric and so requires double the basic quantity of fabric. Patterned or heavier fabrics can be backed with normal lining.

2. The flat width of the valance should be one-and-a-half times the length of the pole.

3. Each section is cut out separately and is complete, without seamlines running through it. As a first step, therefore, it is safest to cut out your shapes in patterns and work out your layout. Design repeats and the width of chosen fabric will make considerable differences to fabric requirements and how the valance is cut out.

4. One complete central section and two partial side sections are ideal for this window. Add more central sections for a wider window, but always retain a complete section in the middle.

5. The central section occupies twice the pole length of the side sections, as they are suspended from their center points; (5) is therefore double (7). To allow the central and side pendants to hang at the same level, the depth of the side section (2) is greater than that of the central section (1). Work out the finished distance from pole to pendant. This will give you the (2) measurement (*a above*).

6. Now calculate (6). To do this, drape a light chain or piece of string from your pole in imitation of the top edge of the central section, from point (8) to point (9). Measure the distance from the pole to the deepest point in the swag; this gives you the (6) measurement. Subtract (6) from (2) and you then have (1).

7. For a simple reckoning for plain fabrics, calculate the top width of each section (based on the top edge being one-and-a-half times the length of the pole that it covers), and assess how many sections can be cut in each width of fabric. Then multiply the number of widths needed by the deepest part of the valance (2), and add an extra ½yd (50cm) for seam allowances and the ties.

8. Allow the same basic quantity of lining fabric as for face fabric.

FITTING

Fix the curtain pole and roller shade fittings. Make sure that the roller will be hidden once the valance is in place.

b

MAKING UP

1. Make a paper pattern of the central section and cut it out twice in fabric so as to allow for the self-lining (b).

c

2. Make a pattern of the side section. Only half of the shape will actually be visible, but allow extra width beyond the center point for the soft wrap-around on each side (c).

3. Cut out two side sections in fabric and two lining pieces.

4. Cut out four ties, each 6in (15cm) wide, and equal to the circumference of the pole plus 6in (15cm) in length in face fabric.

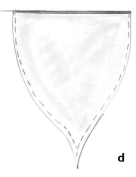

d

5. Pin the pairs of curves right sides together. Baste, and stitch around the curved sides ½in (12mm) from the edge. Clip to relieve tension, turn, and press (d).

6. Turn under the top edge and stitch or slip stitch it closed.

7. Line up the sections side by side and slip stitch the top 2in (5cm) together.

8. Fold the ties lengthwise, right sides together, and stitch along the side and one end. Trim across the corner and turn. Press.

9. Fold the ties in half and pin them along the back of the valance 2in (5cm) below the top edge. The ties are positioned where the central and outer sections meet, and directly above the tips of the outer sections. Slip stitch the ties to the back of the valance.

10. Fold the outer edges back and slip stitch to the back of the outer edges of the valance. Stitch the pendants to the tips (e above).

HANGING

1. Hang the roller shade.

2. Slot the valance onto the pole.

e

PROJECT
Attached Valance

To get the best of both worlds – plenty of light and a generously deep valance – an attached valance is the solution. When the curtains are closed the valance looks like any other. As the curtains draw back, so too does the valance, leaving the window clear. A fringe along the base of the valance will highlight it to great effect. Or you could run a contrasting edging around the valance, the leading edges, and the base of the curtains. Here, a combination of wool fringe and edging provides an effective contrast.

Attached valances are at their best hung from a handsome pole. It is also possible to hang them from a covered cornice board.

The curtains shown here are interlined but this is not essential. Follow the general instructions for interlined or lined curtains for guidance in making the main section of these curtains (see pages 92–5). Sew-on curtain tapes are not suitable for use with attached valances, but there are sometimes sufficient layers to hold the heading up without extra stiffening.

MATERIALS
Face fabric
Lining
Interlining (optional)
Stiffener
Fringe
Contrasting fabric for
  edging

MEASURING
Allow for the flat width of the curtains and the valance sections to be two-and-a-half times their pleated or gathered width.

Valance
The depth of the valance section should be one-fifth of the curtains' overall length plus two seam allowances (face fabric and lining).

Curtains
To finished length add 4in (10cm) for hem and one seam allowance (face fabric and lining). To finished length add 4in (10cm) for hem (interlining).

MAKING UP
1. Cut out the required number of widths for the main curtain in face fabric, lining, and interlining. Cut the widths for the valance section in face fabric and lining.
2. Join the widths for the curtain, then for the valance section. Overlap the widths of interlining, and then join with blind-catchstitch.

3. Lockstitch the free fabric, interlining, and lining, following the instructions for interlined curtains (see page 94). Blind-catchstitch the top edge of interlining to face fabric ½in (12mm) below the top. Leave the top edges of the face fabric and the lining raw.

4. If the fabric is relatively lightweight, insert a strip of stiffener ¾in (19mm) below the top raw edge, between the lining and the interlining. Attach either with blind-catchstitch around all four sides (non-fusible buckram) or fuse layers together using a hot iron to release glue (fusible buckram).

5. Baste through the face fabric and the lining ½in (12mm) below the top edge.

6. Pin the valance face fabric and lining right sides together. Stitch

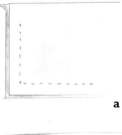

a

b

along the base and up the sides, finishing 4in (10cm) from the top edge (a & b). Then trim the corners, turn, and press.

7. With the right side of the valance against the wrong side of the curtain, pin the valance to the curtain ½in (12mm) from the top edge. Stitch, trim bulk, and press seam open. Remove the basting (c & d).

c

d

8. Fold in the remaining edges of the valance lining and slip stitch into place (e).

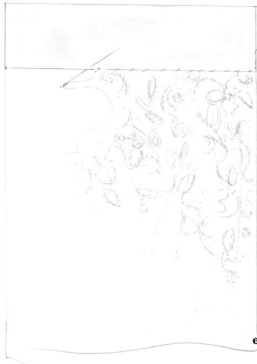

e

9. Pin the contrasting band over the seamline that joins the curtain to the valance and turn in at each end. Slip stitch in place (f).

f

10. Turn the valance over the front of the curtain and baste (g).

g

11. Pleat or gather the heading (see page 97) and then remove the basting.

HANGING
Either insert pin-on hooks or use sew-on hooks attached to a covered band of heading web (see page 98).

Cornices

MATERIALS
Face fabric
Lining
Interlining
Contrasting binding
Small tassels
Heavyweight buckram
  or ¼ in (6mm) plywood
Hook-and-loop tape
Fabric glue and stapler
  (plywood)
Paper (pattern)

FITTINGS
Valance shelf
Brackets
Curtain rod

TOOLS
Drill
Staple gun or hammer
  and tacks
Heavyduty craft knife
  (heavyweight buckram
  backing)
Jigsaw (plywood
  backing)

The terms "cornice" and "valance" are frequently used interchangeably, but a cornice, though often covered with fabric, is usually made of wood, thick cardboard, or buckram. It is firmer and more permanent than a valance, which is always made of fabric. The clean lines of a cornice can be effective where a fabric design might be lost in the folds of a fussier, gathered treatment, and shapes can range from the discreet to the flamboyant. Proportion is crucial; the cornice should balance the rest of the treatment and be in scale with the window.

PROJECT
Gothic Cornice

Often, finding the right shape for a cornice can take longer than its actual construction. In this case, the cornice serves to emphasize, not disguise, the shape of the window, drawing attention to the magnificent pointed arches.

FITTING
1. First, prepare the valance shelf,
2. Staple or tack a line of hook-and-loop tape to the front edge and returns.
3. Attach the curtain rod to the shelf, and the shelf to the wall.

MAKING UP
1. For most windows, buckram is a suitable backing material for a cornice. Plywood, cut with a jigsaw, is better for large-scale schemes or when humidity (in a kitchen or bathroom, for example) would warp the buckram.
2. Cut a pattern from paper. To achieve a symmetrical shape, fold the paper in half before drawing the shape. Always remember to allow for returns, if necessary.
3. Draw the design onto the buckram or plywood and cut it out using a heavyduty craft knife (if using buckram) or with a jigsaw (if using plywood).

4. When cutting out a curve, avoid hesitation, using a steady, sweeping motion. Always have enough materials so that you can try again if necessary.
5. To allow the returns to be bent back easily, score the buckram. Plywood returns should be cut separately and given a hinge by gluing a strip of fabric over the joint.
6. Join the widths of face fabric, and join the widths of lining. Match

the pattern with care – any misalignment will be obvious. Press open seams. The interlining should not be seamed or overlapped, since this would create an uneven surface. It can either be used lengthwise or sections can be laid side by side.
7. Make sure that the cornice has a central panel of fabric with any extra added to either side. Always make sure that the right section of the design shows in the center, so that the

pattern is shown to best effect.
8. Place the pattern in turn on the fabric, lining, and interlining. Cut to shape, allowing an extra 2½ in (6cm) all around for the face fabric, 1½ in (4cm) for the interlining, and ¾ in (19mm) for the lining.
9. Cut out strips of contrasting binding on the cross grain. Fold in half lengthwise and press. Turn under ½ in (12mm) and press again (*a*).

15. Turn the cornice over. Either handsew the tassels to the base

c

of the cornice using tiny stitches, or attach them with fabric glue. Pin the lining to the back, turning in and clipping the overlap. The hook-and-loop tape should run just below the top edge. The lining should be carefully slip stitched into place (*d* below).

d

10. Stitch the hook-and-loop tape to the front of the lining 1in (2.5cm) below its top edge.

a

11. Lay the face fabric, interlining, and buckram face down.
12. Starting at the center top, fold the interlining over the buckram and attach by pressing the seam allowance with a hot iron to release the glue. Do not touch the buckram itself with the iron. If you are using plywood or non-fusible buckram, attach the interlining with fabric glue. Trim away any bulk on the corners and clip

where necessary.
13. Repeat with the face fabric, overlapping the interlining (*b*).
14. Pin the folded edge of the contrasting binding along the cornice, marrying the fold of the binding with

b

the edge of the cornice. Fold the binding at the corners. Using a semi-circular needle, slip stitch into place along the front. Baste the back edge to the fabric seam allowance (*c* above).

16. Press the back of the cornice through the lining to release the glue (fusible buckram).
17. Work a line of prickstitches along the base of the hook-and-loop tape to hold it firmly in position.

Plywood
1. Stitch the hook-and-loop tape to the front of the lining, 1in (2.5cm) below the top edge.
2. Lay the interlining and the plywood face down.

3. Starting from the center top and working outward, turn the top edge of the interlining over to the back of the plywood and staple or tack in position. Repeat for the lower edge.

4. Turn the side edges to the back and staple. Make sure the fabric is not too tight for the returns to swing back.

5. Lay the cornice on the fabric and repeat the stapling process.

6. Place the bias strip along the base edge. It can be either glued or slip stitched along the front to secure it, but should be only lightly glued to the back surface of the plywood.

7. Turn the cornice over. Glue, staple, or tack the tassels into place.

8. Lay the lining over the back.

9. Again starting from the center top, turn under the edges and staple or tack around all four sides, close to the fold, with the staples or tacks parallel to the outer edge. Run a line of staples or tacks below the hook-and-loop tape.

HANGING

1. Mark a center point on the back of the cornice and the front of the board. Marry the center points and join the lines of hook-and-loop tape. If the cornice is particularly heavy, a finishing nail at each end will hold it firmly in place; work the head of the nail behind the fabric (e below).

2. If curtains or shades are to accompany the cornice, make sure that these are hung first.

3. Try to avoid rolling or bending the cornice. If it needs to be rolled, keep the lining facing outward. This prevents any stretching of the face fabric.

e

VARIATION

Plaid Cornice

A double row of piping provides a quietly extravagant finish to this cornice which embodies the three most important themes of this book: scale, simplicity, and appropriateness. The depth of the cornice is in proportion to the length of the curtains; it is generous without being exaggerated. Its line is classic – neither unnecessarily fussy nor dull. Finally, the deeply colored, sober plaid from which the curtains and cornice are made adds just the right note of restraint, providing a gently luxurious backdrop to the room.

VARIATION
Striped Cornice

Cornices do not always have to match the curtains. Here, a bold contrast has been struck (ABOVE) between a striped cornice – edged in cord and finished with multicolored tassels – and floral curtains.

VARIATION
Grecian Urn Cornice

A wide band, juxtaposed with the massive shapes of antique urns, creates a bold effect (LEFT). Despite the different shape, it is made up in the same way as the Gothic cornice in the main project on page 120.

VARIATION
Pagoda Cornice

The top edge of the cornice is a neglected area of design. Almost invariably cornices are given flat tops, while any artistic effort goes into looping lower edges. However, there is ample scope for more interesting outlines if there is room above the window and the cornice does not project far from the wall. The pagoda cornice below does not wrap around the sides and so would leave them exposed.

The shape of this cornice evokes willow-pattern china and fantasies of the Orient. Despite its sober color and black edging, the shape adds a frivolous note to a decorating scheme. The edging emphasizes the pagoda outline, which is set off by a pair of plain white curtains.

This cornice is constructed in just the same way as any other cornice. The curved edging is made using a bias strip of fabric, ironed first to give the central fold and seam allowances. The edging can then be placed over the fabric, giving an equal depth to either side. If only a basic color is required, use dressmaker's bias binding.

A projecting cornice need not rule out such an imaginative treatment, but it calls for action to hide the sides and the workings of the curtain rod. Cover two pieces of buckram or plywood in the cornice fabric and attach them to the side edges of the board.

Cornice Shapes

Lambrequins

Lambrequins were highly fashionable in the last century, but the mention of a lambrequin today usually attracts a blank look. Quite simply, a lambrequin is a glorified cornice. Flat with shaped edges, it extends down the sides of the window. It is made in the same way as a cornice – backed in heavy-weight buckram or plywood – and frames the window, generally extending to sill level. When used alone it is purely ornamental; otherwise, it can hide a roller or Roman shade. A piece of muslin or organdy can be hung inside for a softer look.

Lambrequins offer great opportunity for theatricality, turning the dullest window into a striking feature. For example, converted attics will often have tiny windows that are difficult to curtain, and a lambrequin will give such a window unaccustomed prominence, a hidden shade taking care of the practical business of screening the light. A flamboyant lambrequin might also be appropriate for a single window on a staircase, which is often inaccessible and therefore impractical for raising shades or opening curtains.

Painted Cornice

If your room needs a touch of fantasy, a cut-out cornice – something painted edged in gold, and decorated with alternating blue and gold tassels – might just be the answer! Since this cornice is made of plywood, you should cut out the sides separately and glue a strip of fabric behind adjacent pieces to make a hinge.

Swags

- Formal swags are best used with full-length draperies on large-scale windows.
- Choose the fabric carefully — try to find one that has a natural tendency to drape well.
- Don't be afraid to sacrifice the odd piece of lining fabric for experimental purposes.
- Best results come with swags cut on the cross grain of the fabric, so try to avoid patterned fabrics, or obvious naps, that need to be cut on the straight grain.
- Use the best trimmings that you can afford — swags are lifted by well-matched, good-quality fringes and cords.
- Keep the proportions generous — the depth of swag and length of cascades should balance the length of the draperies and the width of the window.
- Measure with care. A light interlining will help the fabric to drape.
- Nails or long pins and a pinboard ease the task of arranging pleats.

Swags in all different arrangements, have long occupied the center stage of curtain-making. Traditionally associated with heavily draped, large-scale windows, they have recently translated themselves into a multitude of less formal variations.

Formal swags and cascades (the side pieces that cascade down) are made from separate pieces of cloth, individually inter-lined, lined, and pleated, then hung, each in turn, from a valance shelf to create the illusion of continuous drapery. On windows too wide for a single swag, multiple swags are used (see page 13); where they meet is either overlapped or hidden beneath "pipes" or "flutes." The proportions of swags should be generous, and cascades usually need to be about half the overall length of the curtains.

Although it is possible to generalize on the subject of swags, cascades take many different forms. For example, they can be pleated accordion-style, each pleat either hiding the one below or spread out into a line, or they can be made in a spiral, with the fabric rolled up and flattened. Cascades can lie over or under the edges of the swag.

Take care in choosing lining fabrics for tail, pipe, or flute cascades (see page 131). These will play an important part in the color scheme since they are clearly visible in the zigzag lower edges. The lining should complement the face fabric — usually in a paler color — and can be echoed in the choice of trimmings.

The draped pole, made popular by the recent revival of interest in all things Empire, has fooled many a home curtainmaker, whose attempts to reproduce Grecian folds in a single length of cloth have often ended in failure. In fact, these too are best made up from separate sections, with the points where they meet carefully hidden along the top of the pole. Of all the variations, the loose drape (the name for this type is swag) is perhaps the most difficult, often involving complicated asymmetrical sections.

Informal swags — more gathered than pleated, and accessible to one and all — are made from a single piece of cloth, its ends cut into opposing diagonals. They are used simply to soften and enhance the top of the window, usually without curtains or shades, and results can be quick and encouraging. Such arrangements can be interlined, lined, or unlined — many voiles, silks, and laces can be shown off to great effect.

The range for decoration makes swags the subject of some of the most elaborate trimming arrangements. The sweep of the swag can be followed with a line of cording or fringe; the cord can be tied into any number of decorative knots to either side, sometimes weighted down with a pair of handsome tassels, hanging in line with the tails. In fact, fringing is an essential element in every formal swag. Choux, rosettes, bows, and Maltese crosses will give an expensive-looking finish and disguise the points at which the elements join. Lighter, informal swags are generally unsuitable for any trimming heavier than a white pompom fringe or a garland of silk flowers.

A generously proportioned swag (RIGHT), decorated with a subtle fringe and a pair of choux, complements an elegant arched window.

MATERIALS

Swag

Face fabric
Light interlining
Aluminum-coated or
    blackout lining (swag)
Contrasting lining
    (cascades)
Paper or lining (pattern)
Fringe

Curtains

Fabric
Interlining
Lining
Contrasting fabric (for
    leading edge)
Cord
Stiffener (handmade
    heading) or curtain
    tape (machine-stitched
    heading)

FITTINGS

Valance shelf
Curtain rod
Brackets

TOOLS

Covered chain weight
Large pinboard and
    heavyduty pins or fine
    nails (optional)

FITTING

Attach the curtain rod
to the valance shelf,
and then the shelf to
the wall.

PROJECT

Silk Swag and Cascade

Aclassic swag is balanced by cascades finished in choux (see page 127). Tussah silk, a coarse, tough silk, is ideal for this since it drapes well and falls into soft folds. A wide linen fringe links the cream-colored silk with the moss-green damask lining. To avoid an imbalance of translucency between the heavily interlined draperies and lightly interlined swag, block the light that comes through the swag with either aluminum-coated or blackout lining.

The draperies hang straight down from the rod, unencumbered by tiebacks which allows the swag and cascades the prominence they deserve, and provides a welcome vertical line. The padded leading edges with a band of dove-gray cotton, edged in a line of cord, give a discreet air of luxury.

MEASURING AND CUTTING THE PATTERN

see Measuring, page 88.

Swag

1. Hang the covered chain weight from the valance shelf in imitation of the swag's lower edge. The deepest part of the swag should occupy about one-fifth of the overall length from valance shelf to floor. Use this measurement as the base edge of the unpleated swag. The top edge of the unpleated swag should be the length of the valance shelf.

2. Allow for the unpleated depth of the swag to be twice the pleated depth. The base of the flat swag should be given a slight curve in order to help it form an effective swathe.

3. Using the measurements, mark out a pattern. Allow for a seam allowance around the sides and the base of the pattern. Allow a double seam allowance along the top edge of the pattern.

4. Cut out the pattern in lining fabric and pin the pleats (using a pinboard if possible), teasing them into curving, matching drapes. Allow for the curve of the swag to run out at each edge of the board. Trim the sides so that when the lining pattern is flattened, the sides form a zigzag, each of them representing one pleat (a right).

5. For plain fabrics, the swag will be cut on the crossgrain of the face fabric. Obvious patterns, which cannot successfully be tilted at a 45° angle, must be cut on the straight grain instead.

6. If the fabric is not wide enough to take the whole pattern, cut a central section of fabric and add the extra in equal additions to each side. Be sure to run the seams vertically, even if the sections are actually cut on the crossgrain (b right).

7. Allow for an extra strip of fabric the length of the valance shelf plus two seam allowances by a depth of 3½ in (9cm). This serves to bind the top edge of the swag and will also provide the means by which it can be attached

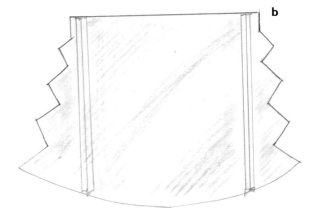

Cascades

❑ The outer edge of each cascade should extend halfway down the curtains. The inner edge is equal to the depth of the swag. The flat width of each cascade is seven times its pleated width, plus the length of the returns, plus an extra 2in (5cm) to turn around the inner edge of the cascade. Calculate for a seam allowance all around. Give the edges a slight flare – in this way the cascade will widen toward the base (c & d, page 129).

Choux
See page 160.

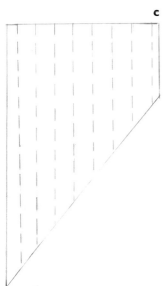

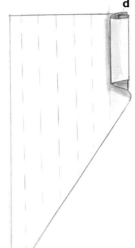

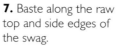

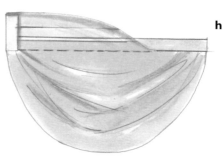

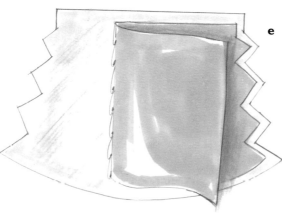

Curtains

❏ The flat width should be two-and-a-half-times the finished gathered width. One length of contrasting fabric will be needed for the leading edge, plus the same length in cord.

❏ Add 2–3in (57.5cm) to the finished length of the curtains for the draped hem.

MAKING UP
Swag

1. Lay the lining pattern on a piece of paper, trace around the edge, and cut out two versions, one with and one without seam allowances. The fabric and lining will be cut with seam allowances, while the interlining will be cut without seam allowances.

2. Using the first pattern, cut out the fabric, on the crossgrain if possible, but on the straight grain if the curtain fabric has any obvious designs or stripes that need to be accommodated. Join the sections together if necessary, and press any open seams.

3. Cut out the interlining and lining on the straight grain. If necessary, turn the interlining or lining on its side to avoid joins.

4. Lay the fabric face down. Lay the interlining over the back of the fabric. Fold back the interlining every 4in (10cm) and work vertical lines of locking stitches, attaching it to the face fabric (e).

5. Fold the base edge of the fabric over edge of interlining and blind-catchstitch (f).

6. Lay the lining face down on the back of the swag, and lock to the interlining in the same way. The lines of locking stitches should end an inch from the base edge to allow the lining to be turned in.

7. Baste along the raw top and side edges of the swag.

8. Turn in the base edge of the lining and slip stitch (g).

9. Pleat the swag and bind the top edge, using the prepared strip. Fold the strip in half lengthwise and turn in seam allowances along the edges and the ends. Press in place. Pin, baste, and slip stitch the band over the top edge of the swag (h above).

10. Attach the fringe to the lower edge.

Cascades

1. Cut out the cascades in fabric and lining, allowing a seam allowance all around. Use the straight grain, being sure to place and match any obvious pattern.

2. Cut the interlining without any seam allowance.

3. Lock the interlining to the fabric and the lining to the interlining in the same way as the swag. Turn in the lining around all four sides.

4. Attach the fringe to the base of each cascade.

5. Pleat, leaving the return free and turning in 2in (5cm) to create a fold along the inner edge (i).

6. Secure the pleats with a line of basting stitches.

Choux

See page 160.

Curtains

❏ Make up as for interlined curtains. Give each edge a 1½in (4cm) border in contrasting fabric. Insert the padded edge (see page 161). Attach cording where the border and main section meet.

HANGING

1. Hang and train the draperies.

2. Position the swag and tack the bound top edge to the top of the shelf.

3. Tack the tails to the front of the shelf.

4. Attach choux.

VARIATION
Swagged Valance

One of the simplest and most attractive ways to decorate the top section of a window is by using a single length of cloth, draped over a pair of hooks supporting a hidden batten.

MATERIALS
Fabric
Lining

FITTINGS
2in (5cm) square-section wood batten
Pair of hooks

TOOLS
Hammer and tacks

FITTING
Mount the batten above the window. Attach the hooks to the window frame below the batten. Make sure that the hooks project enough to carry the swag.

MEASURING
1. Hang leadweight tape, light chain weight, or cord between the hooks in imitation of the swag (see pages 88, 128). Decide on the length of the outer edge of the valance (*1*).
2. Measure the inner-edge of the swag (*2*).
3. Calculate the depth of the swag (*3*) and multiply by two (*a*).

MAKING UP
1. Cut a pattern, allowing a seam allowance on all four sides (*b*).
2. Cut out in the fabric and the lining. Place the two pieces of fabric with right sides together. Pin, baste, and stitch around three sides. Turn and press. Turn in the fourth edge and slip stitch.

HANGING
1. Baste the top of the swag to the top surface of the batten.
2. Lay the swag over the hooks and tease the folds into place.

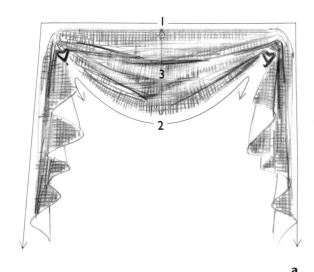

a

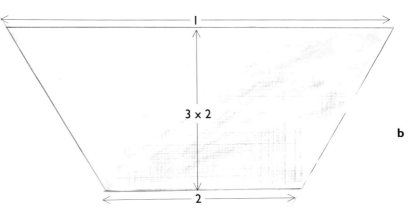

b

VARIATION
Art Deco Swag and Cascades

A modern interpretation of the traditional swag is used here in an original way as an accompaniment to a translucent, striped roller shade. The swag is made in the same way as the main project (page 128) – the difference lies in the small crested tabs that adorn the top section of the cascades. These tabs are made separately and fixed onto the front of the cascades. In keeping with the modernity of the room, the usual rules on swag proportions do not apply.

VARIATIONS
Flutes, Spirals, and Pipes

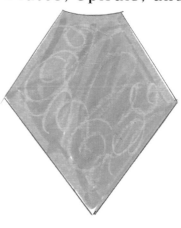

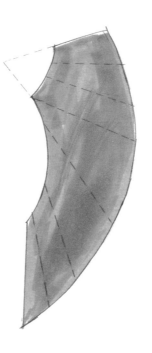

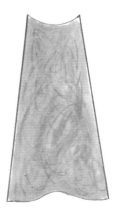

VARIATION

Muslin Swag with Choux

This fan swag is a variation on the more conventional version. It forms the graceful curve typical of the style without masking any of the daylight entering a room. Deeply looped curtains follow the curve of the swag, filtering and diffusing the light. The curtains shown here clear the floor, but could easily be made to floor length. Fat choux punctuate the top edge of the fan, hiding the side edges of the valance shelf.

MATERIALS
Sheer muslin
Hook-and-loop tape or
  tacks
Finishing nails
Lining (pattern)

FITTINGS
Valance shelf (as
  shallow as possible,
  since there are no
  cascades or returns to
  hide the sides of the
  board)
Brackets
Curtain rod
Holdbacks

FITTING
1. Prepare the valance shelf.
2. Attach the curtain rod to the shelf, and the shelf to the wall.
3. Mount the holdbacks in position.

MEASURING
1. Measure the length of the swag (1) using either a leadweight tape or chain weight (see pages 88, 128) (*a below*).
2. Measure the depth of the swag (2) and measure the length of the shelf (3).
3. Make a pattern in the lining fabric, experimenting with relative dimensions. When (3) gathers to form the curve (1), (4) comes up each side to form part of the top edge; (5) is gathered up to form the end points of the swag (*b below right*).

MAKING UP
Swag
1. Allow an extra 1in (2.5cm) all around the pattern. Cut out in the fabric.
2. Make a double ½in (12mm) hem along the base edge and slip stitch in place.
3. Run a line of gathering stitches along (3) and both (5) sections. Draw up gathering threads and secure.
4. Measure and cut a strip of fabric the length of the valance shelf and a width of 3in (7.5cm) to bind the top edge of the swag and provide the means of attachment. If you are using muslin, use plain lining fabric or white cotton twill tape for this job – the muslin is too flimsy.
5. Fold the strip in half lengthwise, turn in a seam allowance along each long edge, and turn in the ends. Press to secure the folds.
6. Place over the top edge of the swag and stitch in place.

7. The swag can be held to the valance shelf using either hook-and-loop tape or tacks. If the first technique is chosen, attach the tape to the back of the bound top edge.

Choux
See page 160.

Curtains
Make up as for unlined curtains (see page 90).

HANGING
1. Hang the curtains and loop them up into the holdbacks.
2. Staple or tack the swag to the top surface and just behind the front edge of the valance shelf. If hook-and-loop tape is used, attach it along the same position on the valance shelf and join it to the back of the swag.
3. Tack the choux to either end around the front corners of the board, using finishing nails.

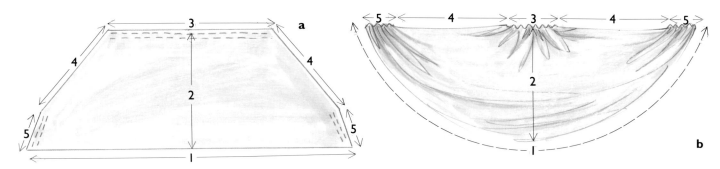

Reefing
Checked Curtains

MATERIALS
Fabric
Lining
Interlining
Weights
Brass or plastic rings

FITTINGS
Pole
Brackets
2x1in (5x2.5cm) board
Screw eyes
Cord
S-ring
Shade pull or tassel
Awning cleat or pair of small knobs

TOOLS
Drill
Awl

Reefed curtains open rather like theater curtains, drawn by a system of cords running through rings sewn in a diagonal line to the back of the curtain. They are practical, decorative, and easy to make: a single pulley insures that both curtains will open evenly; they allow in more light because they are held back at a higher point than curtains held back conventionally; and the vertical sweep is uninterrupted by a tieback.

Reefing is appropriate only with stationary headings and is not suitable for curtains that draw back. With a stationary heading, a decorative motif can be attached to the overlap. Similarly, decorative cording, looped along the heading, remains undisturbed as the curtains are opened and closed.

Stationary rod-pocket curtains offer an opportunity to show decorative finials, while conventional stationary headings allow the use of a curve-fronted valance shelf, giving an elegant bow front to the scheme.

Reefed curtains may crush slightly more than curtains held back by conventional tiebacks, particularly if silk or other delicate fabrics are used. Heavier weights in the hem will help, or the curtains can be kept open, with a shade placed behind.

The weight of a brass shade pull or heavy tassel attached to the end of the cording may result in a continuous dent forming on the leading edge even when the curtains are closed. To prevent this, ease the pressure by tying up the cord.

FITTING

1. Insert three screw eyes into the front of the valance shelf, as shown. Mount the shelf flat on the wall just above the window. Attach the pole just above the shelf.

2. At points (*1*) and (*2*) attach screw eyes to the wall or window frame. These will carry the cord from the edge of the curtains up to the shelf and should be in line with the outer screw eyes (*a*).

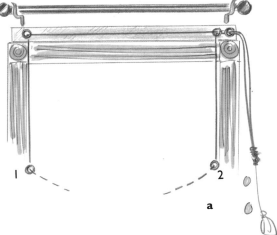

3. Insert an awning cleat or a pair of small knobs about 5in (12cm) apart, on the wall or window frame in line with the pull cord, at about chest height.

MAKING UP

1. Measure and make up the curtains as desired. These rod-pocket curtains hang from a pole. The brackets holding the pole are hidden between the front of the pocket and the pole itself (see page 173).

2. Train the curtains.

3. Use chalk to mark a diagonal line on the back of the curtain folds. This runs from the point on the leading edge where the first ring will be positioned (3), up to the point on the outer edge of the curtain (1) or (2), where a screw eye will lead the cord up to the valance shelf. The distance from (3) to the top of the curtain should be about one-third of the overall length. The distance from (1) and (2) to the top should be about one-quarter to one-fifth of the length (b).

4. Sew rings to the back of each fold using the chalk marks with small stitches and strong thread, and catching all layers.

5. Cut two cords as follows. The shorter cord runs from the leading edge to the outer edge of the curtain, through the screw eye (1) up to the outer screw eye and down to the pull cord (or vice versa if the pull cord hangs on the other side of the window). The longer cord travels much the same path, but runs through the screw eyes on the valance shelf to join its companion on the pull cord side.

6. Knot the cords to the first rings (see page 148) and run them through their paths (c).

7. With the curtains closed and the cords evenly tensioned, sew the raw ends of the cords to the S-ring.

8. Attach a short piece of cord finished with a shade pull or tassel to the other half of the S-ring (see page 151), to hang just below waist height. Use the awning cleat or pair of knobs to anchor the cord.

VARIATION

White Curtains

Here, a dramatic effect has been achieved by also covering the walls between the two windows with curtains. A mounting board has been fixed along the length of wall, with hook-and-loop tape on the front surface. Screw eyes in the base of the board operate the reefing (a below).

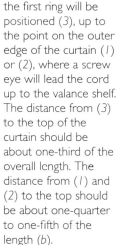

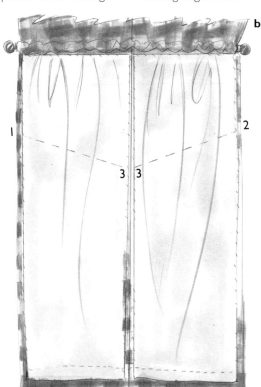

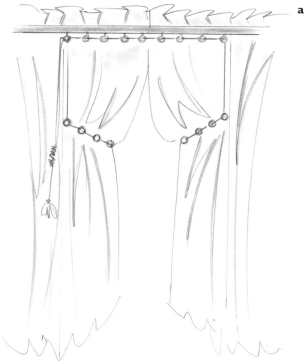

No-Sew Curtains

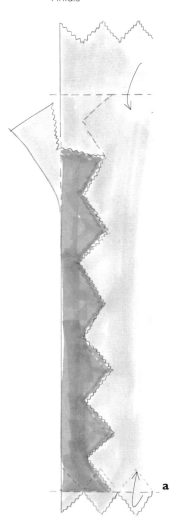

a

MATERIALS
*Fabric (canvas or
   cotton duck)*
Pin-on hooks
Fabric glue
Paper (pattern)

TOOLS
Pinking shears

FITTING
Pole
Brackets
Rings
Finials

There are numerous shortcuts to curtaining a window, and no-sew curtains can be among the most successful. Held together with fabric glue, they take little time or skill to assemble once the shapes are cut.

These curtains are unlined and, to work efficiently, should be made of canvas or cotton duck. A shaped border is cut out in the same fabric, using pinking shears, and glued to the edges of the curtain. The light penetrating the curtain highlights the appliquéd shape, shading from honey color in the center to a deeper caramel at the sides. The top edge can either be an extension to the side border or, as here, be cut into a zigzag and flapped over to form an informal valance. Cut out fish and shell shapes could provide one variation on the no-sew curtain. Flowers, leaves, the sun, or the moon might also provide inspiration.

The simplicity of the design calls for the use of a pole and rings, whether finished off with gilded finials and brass rings or a more austere wrought-iron arrangement. Because canvas or cotton duck is too stiff to form soft drapes, tiebacks will not work, so the curtains are not trained into formal pleats.

If possible, no-sew curtains should be made from a single width of fabric. Cotton duck and canvas are available in much bigger widths than regular fabrics, wide enough to cover all but the very largest windows. This treatment lacks the pleating or gathering of conventional curtains – much of their appeal lies in the gently wavy surface – so the flat curtain width is about one-and-a-half times the length of the pole that it occupies.

No-sew curtains are most suited to the bedroom – it is a delight to wake up to sunlight filtered through the appliquéd shapes.

MEASURING
❑ Width: The flat width should be one-and-a-half times the length of pole that the curtain occupies. There are no side hems, so nothing need be added. Joining widths is not really advisable with such heavy fabric, and the see-through pattern would be spoiled by a visible seam, so try to find fabric of the right width. If there is no other solution, however, overlap the widths by 1in (2.5cm) and either glue

together or run a double line of stitches.
❑ Length: Add 6in (15cm) for the hem and one-fifth of the finished curtain length for valance flap.
❑ Side borders: One extra width of fabric.

FITTING
Mount the pole and finial.

MAKING UP
1. Prepare a paper pattern of:
* Border shape
* Hem zigzag
* Valance zigzag
(see page 148).

2. Cut the length.
3. Cut the side borders to the finished length plus 2in (5cm) to turn under the hem. Allow 1in (2.5cm) extra on the width to wrap around the side edge of the main panel.
4. Lay the main panel face down. Cut the zigzag in the hem.
5. Turn up the hem and glue sparingly. Always avoid using excess glue as this will show through, discolor, and cause a range of other problems.
6. Turn the curtain over and position the

side panels to overlap the edges by 1in (2.5cm) and the hem by 2in (5cm) (*a* left).
7. Glue into place. Do not allow any glue to seep from under the border.
8. Turn over the valance flap and secure with intermittent dabs of glue (*b* right).

HANGING
Position pin-on hooks along the back and hang (*c* right).

b

c

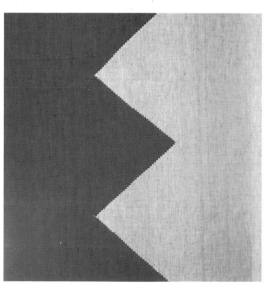

Border Shapes

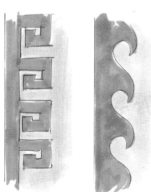

Tiebacks

Most often, curtains are seen at their best gently draped into tiebacks, forming a graceful frame to the window. It takes some effort to wrap the tiebacks around the curtains each morning, teasing the folds into place, but the effort is well rewarded. If you wish to retain the elegant folds of a newly hung curtain, you could leave the curtains permanently tied back, drawing down a hidden roller shade for seclusion at night.

Tiebacks take many forms, ranging from decorative chains or a pair of tassels on a braided cord, to ruffles or simple, stiffened tiebacks made in the same fabric as the curtain. You will probably need to experiment to find the best position for tiebacks. They are conventionally set about two-thirds of the way to the floor. However, you may wish to make your window look taller by positioning the tiebacks lower – or they may look best lined up with the windowsill. Try to avoid placing them exactly halfway down.

Positioning the tiebacks fairly high up will create an effect similar to reefing (see page 134), letting in more light than when placed lower down. You may prefer to line the tiebacks in the face fabric so that even when they are hanging down at night with the curtains closed, they never show a plain lining.

Remember that the hooks or other fixings at the sides of the window will not necessarily be at the same height; cord tiebacks, for example, hang almost vertically.

A crescent tieback with a contrast band (LEFT) unobtrusively retains the graceful folds of a matching curtain.

Crescent Tieback

The cresent-shaped tieback is the most conventional means of tying back a pair of curtains. Its curved shape and broad center provide a firm hold and cause minimum wrinkling. Make sure that the tieback is not too tight or too loose – it should hug the curtain, neither squeezing it into a series of wrinkles nor flapping against a limp leading edge. The key to a pair of elegant curtains – the uniform folds hanging in regimented lines – is a pair of generous tiebacks.

Tiebacks and curtains are usually made in the same fabric. Welting can be in this fabric. For greater prominence, a contrasting welting, edging, or ruffle might echo a color taken from the fabric itself or from the rest of the room. For further decoration, rosettes, choux, and bows can be sewn to the front of tiebacks and the lower edge can be cut into a decorative shape – a double curve or scallops, for example. A shaped lower edge often precludes welting, which is difficult to fit around the tight curves.

Most tiebacks attach to the tieback hooks by means of brass rings or D-rings. This project shows a tieback anchored with ribbons made up in the contrasting fabric (FAR LEFT).

MATERIALS FOR TIEBACKS
Face fabric
Interlining
Lining
Buckram
Contrasting fabric
Paper (pattern)
Brass or plastic rings

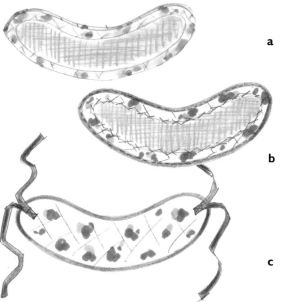

a

b

c

MAKING UP
1. Measure around the finished curtain to assess length of tieback.
2. Using a pattern, cut out the shape first in buckram. Cut out again in face fabric, lining, and interlining, overlapping the pattern by 1 in (2.5cm).
3. Overlap the interlining by ½in (12mm) (fusible buckram).
4. Stretch the interlining, then the face fabric, around the buckram, clipping and trimming to avoid bulk. Press seam allowances with a hot iron (fusible buckram) (*a*). Blind-catchstitch into place (non-fusible buckram).

5. Cut a bias strip. Fold in half lengthwise; press. Turn in one edge; press. Lay central fold along edge of tieback. Pin along turned edge and slip stitch. Baste back edge to fabric turning (*b*).
6. Place the lining over the back of the tieback and fold in around the edges. Slip stitch. Press with a hot iron to fuse (fusible buckram).

7. For the ties, cut four strips of fabric twice the desired finished length and twice the finished width, plus two seam allowances. Fold each in half lengthwise, right sides together, and stitch around the long side and one end. Trim, turn, and press. Turn in and sew the open end. Fold each in half and sew to tieback (*c*).

Ruched Tieback

A ruched tieback is a simple alternative to the stiffened tieback with contrasting band also described on this page. Its fat ruffles give an attractively informal finish to a pair of curtains. This type of tieback works best with lightweight curtains.

MAKING UP
1. Cut a strip of buckram to the finished length.
2. Cut a strip of face fabric and one of interlining to twice the finished length and four times the finished width, plus two seam allowances.
3. Lay the interlining over back of fabric and treat as one layer.

4. Fold the strip of fabric and interlining in half, right sides together. Stitch around the long side and one end (*d* below). Clip the corner and turn.
5. Insert the buckram into the tube and gather up evenly. Turn in the open end and slip stitch. Prickstitch across each end. Sew on a ring.

d

Ruffle-Trimmed Tieback

A plain, crescent-shaped tieback is enhanced with a knife-pleated ruffle, creating a more tailored look than with a gathered ruffle.

MAKING UP

1. Make up as for the crescent tieback, but omit the edging. Before lining, slip stitch a pleated ruffle to the back (e).

2. Lay the lining over the back and slip stitch into position. Sew on rings instead of ties in order to attach the tieback to the hooks.

e

Pleated Tieback

Simple yet elegant, this unusual tieback is made from a rectangle gathered into narrow accordion pleats. It would look particularly attractive echoing the heading of a pencil-pleated curtain.

MAKING UP

1. Cut the buckram to finished length.
2. Cut fabric to twice finished width plus seam allowances and to finished length plus seam allowances.
3. Fold in half lengthwise, right sides together, and machine-stitch along the side and one end. Trim corner, turn, and press.

4. Insert the buckram. Turn in the open end and slip stitch.
5. Stitch four parallel lines the length of the tieback.

6. Gather up into neat pleats and prickstitch in place.
7. Sew a ring to each end of the tieback (f).

f

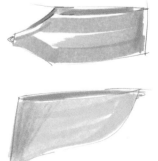

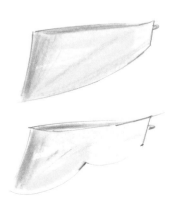

Tieback Shapes

Pocket Tieback

The intricate folded surface of this tieback appears to have been invented by either an origami expert or a napkin folder from an expensive French restaurant. The result is charming and the crisp pleats are a perfect foil to the flat surfaces of the curtain beneath.

MAKING UP
1. Cut out a strip of face fabric and one of lining to the width of the tieback plus two seam allowances by three times the finished length.
2. With right sides together, stitch around three sides, leaving one end open. Clip the corners and turn. Press, turn in the open end, and slip stitch across.
3. Form into regular box pleats (see page 183). Stitch down the back of each pleat (*g*).
4. Attach the edges of the box pleats to one another with a stitch one-third in from the top (*1*) and another the same distance from the base (*2*) (*h*).
5. Fold back the center of the top and base edge of each pleat and secure with a few small stitches (*3*) (*i*). Stitch a ring to each end.

g

h

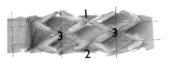

i

Roses Tieback

Yellow velvet roses and green velvet leaves, set against a printed velvet curtain, provide an irresistible combination of colors and texture. Made with a simple tieback as its base, the skill in this project lies in fashioning the roses and, to a lesser extent, the leaves.

j

MAKING UP
1. Take a strip of fabric 8in (20cm) wide and 34in (86cm) long, preferably of velvet or velveteen. Fold in half lengthwise. Cut a wedge from the raw edge so fabric measures 1in (2.5cm) wide at one end, 8in (20cm) at the other (*j*).
2. Starting at the narrow end of the folded fabric, which forms the center of the rose, make a cartwheel spiral, twisting and bunching the fabric to make "petals" (*k*).

k

3. Tuck the raw end behind the rose and hand sew the spiral into place.
4. Repeat to make the smaller roses, using strips of fabric up to one-half the size of the first rose.

5. Cut out leaf-shaped pieces of fabric measuring 3 x 2in (7.5 x 5cm). Place right sides together and stitch around two-thirds of the edge, close to raw edge (*l*).

l

6. Trim the seams and turn. Insert pliable wire into the seamline around the outer edge. Baste wire into place.
7. Zigzag stitch along the edges and up the middle of the leaves. Straight stitch fanning lines in imitation of the leaves' natural veins (*m*).
8. Gently form the leaves into natural-looking shapes.

m

9. The roses and leaves are attached to a crescent tieback (see page 139) before the lining is sewn to the back. The tieback should, however, be made unusually narrow so as not to be visible behind the roses. Then stitch the roses and the leaves to both the front and side of each tieback.

Shades

Ashade is a single piece of fabric, raised by means of a spring mechanism or cording system. It can be ruched into festoons; it can be gathered into a balloon shade; or it can be flat against the window, either rolling up or rising into a series of horizontal pleats.

Shades are wonderfully versatile – they can block out all light or operate as filters for daylight. They can be hidden away beneath a cornice or pair of curtains, or serve as the decorative focus themselves. They can be plain and unobtrusive or show a bold design.

Since a shade need cover only the window itself, it is often a useful treatment where there is insufficient room for a curtain to stack back to either side. Similarly, if small children with dirty fingers or splashes from a sink are likely to cause problems, a shade will pull up out of the way. If a window seat causes an obstruction, one or more shades, ending at the level of the window sill, will cover the window most effectively.

A balloon shade, and, to a lesser extent, a Roman shade, will always obscure a window's top section – this is a problem that can be partially overcome by raising the mounting board slightly. (Care should be taken not to make the shade look detached from the window, however.) A roller shade is the only type of shade that clears the window entirely.

Aesthetically, shades can be adapted to any setting. Sleek Roman shades complement the clean lines of a modern apartment, while a balloon shade could look good in a historic town house, and a roller shade made of checked gingham would find a perfect setting in a rural farmhouse.

PROJECT
Roller Shades

Roller shades offer a wide range of possibilities, from the purely functional to the highly decorative. By varying the shape of the lower edge, using large designs or geometric patterns, painting, or stenciling, the roller shade can be adapted to suit a multitude of settings.

Close-weave fabrics such as cotton are suitable for roller shades when used with a stiffening spray (loose-weave fabrics tend to lose their shape). Pre-stiffened fabric and fusible shade backing are also available.

Bear in mind that a shaped lower edge will be completely functional only if hung outside the window frame clearing the sill.

MATERIALS
Fabric and stiffening spray or pre-stiffened shade fabric
Bias binding or contrasting fabric
Slat
Paper (pattern)

FITTINGS
Roller shade kit
Shade pull

TOOLS
Carpenter's level

FITTING
Screw the brackets supplied with the kit into position, making sure they are perfectly aligned. This is one of the few fittings that requires a carpenter's level to guarantee a perfect horizontal.

MAKING UP
Pre-stiffened fabric
This will not ravel when cut. Be sure to cut precise right-angled corners.

Unstiffened fabric
1. Cut fabric, allowing an extra 12in (30cm) in width and 18in (46cm) in length (the stiffening spray will cause shrinkage).
2. Hang the fabric in a well-ventilated place, and spray both sides evenly. Leave to dry thoroughly.
3. Cut to size. Allow an extra 1in (2.5cm) to the width for side hems and add 12in (30cm) to the finished length.

Shaped base
1. Make a pattern (see page 115). Cut out the shaped base, matching any pattern with the top section and allowing for the same side hems. Allow for a generous overlap with the main section. This will form the casing for the slat.
2. Cut a bias strip in the unstiffened contrasting fabric or bias binding to the width of the shade plus hems.
3. Glue or stitch the bias strip or binding to the base shape.

4. Make side hems in both sections and zigzag into position.
5. Overlap the top and base sections. Make two horizontal lines of machine stitching close to the overlap edges, forming a casing to take the slat (*a*).

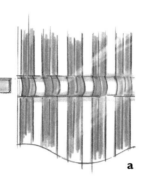

a

6. Cut the slat 1in (2.5cm) shorter than the finished width, and insert. Slip stitch across the ends of the casing.
7. Screw the shade pull to the center point of the slat through the fabric (*b*).

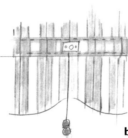

b

8. Lay the roller on the right side of the shade's top edge. A guideline will help to achieve a straight line. Baste the top edge of the shade to the roller (*c*).

c

Straight base
1. Make a double hem large enough to accommodate the slat. Insert the slat and slip stitch across the ends of the casing (*d*).

d

2. Screw the shade pull to the center point of the slat through the fabric.

HANGING
Roll the shade onto the roller. Insert the roller into the brackets.

Alternative Shapes

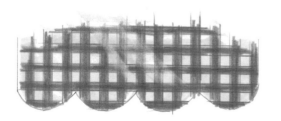

VARIATION
Roll-Up Shade

This shade is made from an unlined check gingham, and is lowered or raised by means of screw eyes and cording. Unlike a roller shade, it rolls up from the bottom rather than the top and does not have a spring mechanism. Accompanied by a graceful swag of sheer white fabric draped over the valance shelf, this simple, unsophisticated shade seems perfect for its surroundings. A single coat hook or awning cleat will anchor the cords in position.

It is always best to use lightweight fabrics for this project – anything heavier would prove too cumbersome. Keeping a small roll of material at the base of the shade facilitates the rolling process.

MATERIALS
Fabric
¾in (19mm) dowel
Hook-and-loop tape

FITTINGS
Valance shelf
Brackets
Screw eyes
Coat hook or awning
  cleat
Shade cord
Brass or wood shade
  pull
S-ring

MEASURING
❑ Width: The finished width should be equal to that of the window. Add 2in (5cm) for the side hems.
❑ Length: The finished length should be 4in (10cm) longer than the

a

space itself (the shade retains a base roll). Add 3¾in (9.5cm) for the lower hem and top hem.

FITTING
1. Staple a line of hook-and-loop tape along the top of the valance shelf, close to the front edge.
2. Fix screw eyes to the base of the valance shelf at the points where the cords will attach.
3. Using an awl, prepare the holes for the screw eyes in the front of the shelf. Two should be in line with the screw eyes below. The third should be on the pull-side of the shade, above the anchor point (a) below).
4. Fit the valance shelf onto the brackets. Fix the coat hook or awning cleat to the anchor point.

MAKING UP
1. Cut the required number of widths and join using flat fell seams. If more than one width is involved, be sure to have a central panel.
2. Turn in double ½in (12mm) side hems and stitch close to the fold.
3. Make a single 2¾in (7cm) bottom hem, and fold the hem in half to form the dowel pocket. Stitch close to the fold (b).

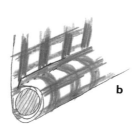

b

4. Make a double ½in (12mm) top hem and stitch close to the fold.
5. Stitch a line of hook-and-loop tape to the back of the heading.
6. Cut the dowel to length, ¾in (19mm) short of the finished width of the shade. Insert the dowel into the pocket and slip stitch across each end.

HANGING
1. Join the lines of hook-and-loop tape.
2. Knot each cord to the appropriate screw eyes on the base of the valance shelf (see page 149).
3. Pierce the fabric with the awl at the three screw eye positions on the front of the valance shelf, taking care not to break the fibers but instead pushing the weave apart, so that the screw eyes will not twist the fabric.

4. Insert the three screw eyes into the front of the valance shelf, through the shade, using the prepared awl holes. Slot the cords through the screw eyes (c).
5. Roll the base section of the shade.

c

6. Holding the shade in a perfect horizontal, trim and knot the cords and attach them to an S-ring (see page 151).
7. Thread the single cord coming out of the base of the S-ring cord through a brass or wood shade pull and knot the end.

Shades
Roman Shades

MATERIALS
Face fabric
Lining
Interlining
Dowels
Hook-and-loop tape

FITTINGS
Mounting board
Brackets (optional)
Screw eyes
Awning cleat
Shade cord
Brass or wood
 shade pull
S-ring

TOOLS
Drill
Staple gun or hammer
 and tacks
Awl

A Roman shade is basically a flat piece of fabric, backed by a line of parallel, horizontal bars, which pulls up on cords to form neat, regular folds.

These shades take many forms. When lined and interlined they have all the thermal qualities of curtains. If backed with a black-out lining, they will exclude light; if unlined they will filter sunlight, while retaining privacy. When pulled up during the day, they permit uninterrupted daylight – and are out of the way of cats and children.

Bordered, fringed, painted, or plain, Roman shades can stand on their own or be stacked away behind a cornice. They can hang inside or outside the window frame, but will become unwieldy if wider than 4ft 9in (1.4m). In such cases, it is as well to increase the number of shades.

Roman shades are economical with fabric and will show off the fabric design to best advantage. Once in place, the cording should prove efficient and predictable, though in time it will need to be replaced.

FITTING
1. The mounting board should be deep enough to allow a line of screw eyes to be inserted between the front surface of the shade and the wall or window frame. However, since a Roman shade has no returns, the board should also be as shallow as possible. There is a danger that the edge of the board will be visible and that the shade will hang away from the window, letting in light and drafts around the sides.
2. The fittings will be taking considerable strain and should therefore be firmly attached to the wall or window frame. Most shades will hang from 2 x 2in (5 x 5cm) boards, which can be

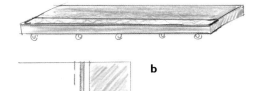

a

b

screwed into the wall or ceiling. If greater depth is needed, a board can rest on brackets mounted on either side of the window. The fittings are usually positioned resting on the wood trim around the window.
3. Cut the mounting board to the appropriate length and prepare it.
4. Run a line of screw eyes along the base of the mounting board. Most Roman shades

have two or three lines of cords running vertically up the back and each line should have a screw eye directly above it.
5. Staple or tack hook-and-loop tape along the top of the mounting board, slightly behind the front edge. If it is mounted on the ceiling, staple the tape along the front edge (*a & b*).
6. Mount an awning cleat into the wall at a point where the cords can be tied.

MEASURING
❑ Width: The finished width should be equal to the width of the window. Add 2½in (6cm) for side hems.
❑ Length: Extra length is needed for the strip of hook-and-loop tape if it runs along the top of the mounting board.
❑ Fabric and interlining: Add 8in (20cm) for hems.
❑ Lining: Allow extra length for the lining, since it will be folded and stitched to form horizontal pockets for the dowels. Multiply the length of each pocket by the number of dowels needed up the back of the shade.
❑ Allow approximately 8in (20cm) between dowels, depending on the size of the window, and calculate how many will run across

5. Fold the lining so that the seam lines match. Baste and then

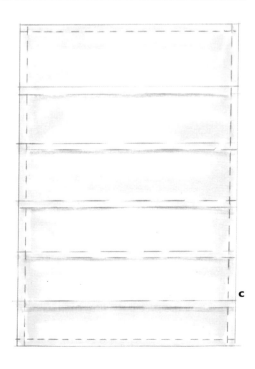

d

stitch them together. Press (*d*).

6. Lay down the face fabric and interlining.

7. Turn up a 4in (10cm) hem in the fabric and interlining to run in line with the lowest dowel. Fold over the side and top hems and press.

8. Using the pressing lines as a guide, trim the interlining around the top and sides so that the raw edge fits neatly into the hems.

9. Blind-catchstitch the hem and slip stitch the edges (no miter is needed).

10. Position the lining on the back of the shade. Turn under at the top and bottom, pin around all four sides and through all the thicknesses, just above the dowel lines. Baste into place. Slip stitch around edges.

11. Stitch the dowel lines. Make sure that the machine tension is right and the thread matches the fabric.

12. Run hook-and-loop tape behind the top of the shade. Stitch in place.

13. Insert the dowels into the pockets and slip stitch across end.

the back of the shade. Allow approximately 4in (10cm) between the lowest dowel and the lower edge of the shade. For example, if there are ten dowels with 3in (7.5cm) needed to hold each one (they should fit snugly but not tightly), add 30in (70cm) plus two seam allowances to the finished length of the lining.

MAKING UP
1. Cut out the face fabric and the interlining to the appropriate size.

2. Use flat-fell seams to join widths of fabric and lining.

3. Turn in the side edges of the lining twice by ¾in (19mm) – 1½in (3.8cm) in total on each side. Stitch along the edge of this hem close to the fold.

4. Making sure that the seams are strictly parallel and at right angles to the sides, mark the dowel pockets on the lining front (c right).

c

14. Using strong thread, sew rows of rings to the dowel pockets. Three rows – one up the center and one 2in (5cm) in from each edge – are sufficient; add more if the shade is unusually wide (e below).

cord. Insert the first noose through the end ring and slot the other end of the cord through the noose. Pull tight (*f* right). In this way you will make sure that the cord will be firmly attached and the knot cannot become

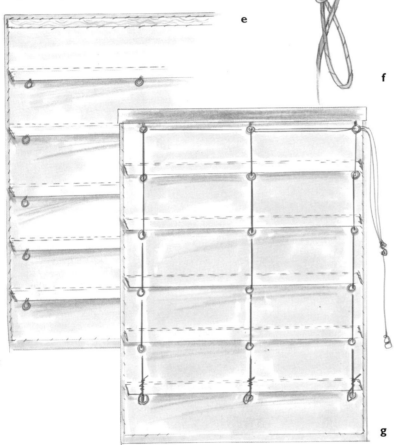

e

f

g

VARIATION
Zigzag Roman Shade and Matching Cornice

A bound zigzag edge on both shade and cornice, finished with a row of tiny tassels, gives a dashing finish to an otherwise conventional room. The cornice is made with a buckram backing; the Roman shade is soft, with only one slat above the bottom panel.

CORDING AND HANGING
1. Lay the shade face down. Decide on which side you wish the pull-cord to hang.
2. Starting from their respective points on the base of the shade, train the cords through the rings, across the back of the heading, and down to the point where they will join the S-ring. Cut each to length. Make a hangman's noose about ¾in (19mm) long in the end of each

loose. Repeat the process for the remaining cords.
3. Join the lines of hook-and-loop tape.
4. Thread the cords through the screw eyes attached to the base of the shade mounting board.
5. Holding the cords taut with perfectly even tension, and making sure that the shade is hanging straight, insert the cords through one-half of the S-ring. Stitch into place, disguising it with

a spiral of cord which is also secured with stitches. Run a single cord off the other part of the S-ring, disguising this in the same way (see page 151) (*g*).
6. Thread the end of the cord through the shade pull, and knot the cord to secure it.
7. Pull up the shade and secure it by wrapping the cord around the awning cleat attached to the wall.

MATERIALS
Shade
Face fabric
Lining
Contrasting fabric
¾in (19mm) cotton tape
Tassels
Hook-and-loop tape
Brass or plastic rings
Slat
Mounting board
Awning cleat
Paper (pattern)

Cornice
Face fabric
Lining
Contrasting fabric
Interlining
Buckram
Hook-and-loop tape
Valance shelf
Brackets

FITTING
1. Mount a valance shelf on strong brackets above the window. Hook-and-loop tape along the front will hold the cornice in place.
2. To the base of the valance shelf and 1¼in (3cm) behind the front edge, fix a square-section mounting board. Staple or baste hook-and-loop tape to the front edge. Run a line of screw eyes along the base for the cording (a).

a

3. Fix an awning cleat to the wall or window to anchor the cording.

MAKING UP
Shade
1. Cut the face fabric and lining to the correct length and width of the window plus one seam allowance all around. Allow for the zigzag shape to hang below the window sill.
2. Using a pattern, cut out a zigzag shape along the base of the face fabric and lining.
3. Pin the fabric and lining right sides together along the sides and base. Baste and stitch, allowing ¾in (19mm) for seams.
4. Turn, trimming and clipping as necessary, and press flat.
5. Cut a bias strip in the contrasting fabric (see page 182). Fold in half lengthwise, make side hems, and press. Slip stitch the bias strip along the lower edge.
6. Stitch on the tassels.
7. Run parallel vertical lines of cotton tape up the back of the shade, from the top of the slat pocket to within ¾in (19mm) of the top, raw edge. Prickstitch up the center of the tapes, penetrating both of the layers.
8. Mark the positions of the rings on the tapes. They should be in line with each other, at 8–12in (20–30cm) intervals. With the first ring attached to the top of the pocket, sew the rings onto the shade using strong thread. All but the lowest rings should go through both layers.
9. Make a ¾in (19mm) hem along the top. Stitch a line of hook-and-loop tape to cover.
10. Cut a strip of lining fabric to accommodate the slat in the necessary width plus two generous seam allowances. Its length is the finished width of the shade plus two seam allowances.
11. Turn in the ends of the lining strip. Stitch close to the raw edge.
12. Pin into position, turning in side edges.
13. Stitch close to the upper, and then the lower, folds.
14. Cut the slat 1in (2.5cm) shorter than the finished width of the shade, and insert into the pocket. Slip stitch across both ends (b below).

HANGING
See page 148.

Cornice
A matching zigzag cornice, backed with plywood or buckram and given coordinating banding, completes the scheme. For making up, see page 120.

b

VARIATION
"Stained Glass" Shade
As the daylight penetrates, this paper-thin, translucent shade lights up in the manner of a stained glass window. The loose weave of the pure white linen allows the shade to screen the window without excluding the light – a highly decorative and original alternative to the conventional glass curtain. It may be used either for reasons of privacy or simply as adornment.

The basic principle behind the shade's construction is the same as the lining of a normal Roman shade (see page 146). The fabric sections are overlapped and stitched, and the shade is then folded and stitched to form the dowel pockets.

Balloon Shades

MATERIALS
Face fabric
Lining
Interlining
Fusible buckram
Weights
Narrow cotton tape
Fringe
Braid
Tassel
Shade cord
Brass or plastic rings
Hook-and-loop tape

FITTINGS
Valance shelf or
  mounting board
Brackets
Screw eyes
Two small brass or
  wood knobs (or a
  coat hook)
S-ring

TOOLS
Drill
Awl
Staple gun or hammer
  and tacks

In recent years the balloon shade has become very popular. In fact, the simple pull-up curtain on which it is based has been in common use since the eighteenth century, and was one of the earliest forms of curtaining used.

The example here is a copy of a curtain at Osterley Park, near London, famous for its mid-eighteenth-century interior. The house illustrated belongs to much the same period, and the window treatment provides an ideal solution for its paneled hall.

At night the shade becomes, in effect, a curtain, dropping to floor length and losing its billowing festoons. Heavy weights at the base of each line of rings make it extremely simple to operate. The cord is wound around two knobs in a figure-eight.

A balloon shade is not difficult to make. This facsimile example is raised through an ingenious wheel system and has specially cast pear-shaped lead weights along the lower edge, but standard screw eyes and curtain weights make excellent substitutes.

Once lowered, the shade takes on the appearance of a graceful curtain, grazing the floor. In contrast, when pulled up to its daytime position, it forms billowing festoons, and the decorative purpose of the fringe becomes apparent.

FITTING

1. Prepare the valance shelf or mounting board.
2. Insert screw eyes along the base to take the cording, one for each vertical line of cord and one slightly in from the edge on the pull-up side.
3. Staple or tack hook-and-loop tape to the front edge and returns of the shelf or board. Mount, using brackets, or screw it directly into the wall or ceiling.
4. Fix a pair of small knobs, about 10in (25cm) apart (or one coat hook) into the wall at chest height, in line with the pull cord to hold the cording.

MEASURING

❏ Width: The flat, unpleated width should be two-and-a-half times the finished width. Add 4in (10cm) for hems.
❏ Length: The fringe should graze the floor and the heading should project 2in (5cm) above the shelf or board. Add 8in (20cm) for hems.
❏ Fringe and braid: These should extend along the width of the hem and one-quarter of the distance up each side.

MAKING UP

1. Cut and join the widths of face fabric and lining. Press and trim the seams.
2. Cut a 3in (8cm) strip of interlining and fusible buckram. Insert into the heading, folding over the top and sides of the face fabric. Baste in place.
3. Cut an 8in (20cm) strip of interlining and

insert into hem (*a*).
4. Fold in the sides and hem, and secure using blind-catchstitch.
5. Turn up and stitch the hem of the lining.
6. Lay the lining over the face fabric, wrong sides together. Leave a ¾in (19mm) gap all around. Pin and stitch around all four sides.
7. Press the heading with a hot iron to release the glue from the fusible buckram.
8. Mark the positions of the cotton tape with parallel lines up the central section, about 8in (20cm) apart.
9. Pin and prickstitch the lines of tape through all layers, starting 6in (15cm) from the baseline. To save time, make your prickstitches at least 1in (2.5cm) long.
10. Mark the positions of the rings on the

tape lines. They should be in line horizontally, and spaced at approximately 6in (15cm) intervals. Sew into place.
11. Stitch several weights into lining bags. Sew the bags into place at each corner and at the base of each vertical line of rings (*b*).
12. Hand sew the fringe and braid into position.
13. Pleat the heading by hand, and baste. Stitch a line of hook-and-loop tape to the back of the heading 2in (5cm) from the top edge. Remove the basting stitches (*c*).

c

HANGING

1. Cut the cords to length (about one and a half times the length of the curtain, plus their distances across the top), tie each to the lowest ring (see page 148) and run them through the rings.
2. Join the lines of hook-and-loop tape on

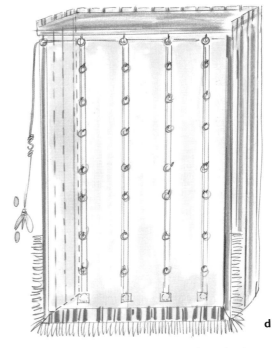
d

the curtain and valance shelf or board (*d*).
3. Feed the cords through the screw eyes. With the shade down and equal tension in all the cords, sew the ends to the S-ring. Coil cord around seam; sew in place.
4. Cut another piece of cord, attaching the tassel or shade pull to one end and the S-ring to the other. Finish with another coil (*e*).
5. To hold the curtain in a raised position, wind the cord around the pair of knobs in a figure-eight (*f*).

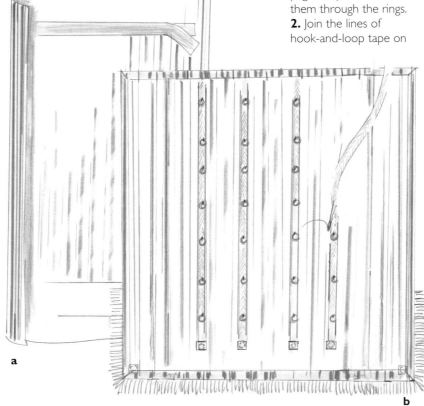
a

b

e

f

VARIATION
Yellow Silk Balloon Shade

This balloon shade is made in much the same way as the balloon shade already described. However, instead of the heading being pleated across its width, two large inverted pleats are placed directly above the lines of cording. Although the shade is not intended to drop to the floor, in order for it to retain its looped lower edge, even at level, extra length is needed – about 10in (25cm) below the sill is usually sufficient.

VARIATION
Child's Shade

A small child lying in bed will take pleasure from any object that moves, reflects light, or makes a noise. This shade does all that and more. It is really no more than a simple balloon shade, but small bells tied to its cording rings chime as the breeze blows through the window or when the shade is raised and lowered. An assortment of seashells sewn to the front jangle and pick up the light, while a row of toy birds stare out from their perches on the top of the valance shelf. When the child tires of the arrangement, other objects can be substituted. Try tiny toys, silk flowers, buttons, or foreign coins instead of shells, or replace the birds with a line of brightly colored paper flags.

MAKING UP
1. Make up in the same way as a balloon shade (see page 150), but allow for the shade, when fully extended, to end 10in (25cm) below the sill.
2. Lay the shade flat and work out the positions of the shells. Using the finest drill bit, pierce holes in the shells. Sew the shells onto the front of the shade itself.
3. Tie bells to the rings up the back.
4. Hand sew length of braid along top edge.
5. Pleat the shade and stitch a line of hook-and-loop tape to the back of the heading.

HANGING
1. Join the line of hook-and-loop tape on the shade to the front edge of the shelf.
2. These birds are made of plastic foam, held in position by tooth picks inserted between the heading and shelf.
3. Avoid objects that can be easily pulled off and swallowed by a small child. Sew on very securely to ensure safety.

VARIATION
Fan Shade

A single line of rings and cord up the center back of this sheer muslin
shade pulls it up to form a pair of fan-shaped cascades.

Paint Effects

Decorating your own fabric is a highly satisfying start to any project, particularly if there is a touch of the frustrated artist in you. Whether you stencil, print, or paint, you have control over the patterns and the colors, and walls and other surfaces can be matched, imitated, or blended with precision.

Inexpensive cottons provide the basis for any number of techniques, and the scope for experimentation is without limit – be warned, it can become a passion. Do not be afraid to stray beyond the pre-cut stencil: try a little freehand work, putting together your own designs.

Stenciling

A few simple do-it-yourself paint effects can completely transform a plain piece of natural cloth, be it cotton, linen, or silk. The most straightforward of these is probably stenciling, and a huge range of stencil shapes is available, in books and pre-cut, from the plainest star shapes to amazingly elaborate patterns. Even more intricate, three-dimensional patterns can be built up using one or more stencils, each in a different color.

For the more adventurous, stenciling can be used in conjunction with hand painting. This allows you to soften the stencil's hard outline and gives scope for a structured yet hand-crafted finish.

The basic principle of stenciling is simple: a shape is cut in cardboard, this is laid on the fabric, and, by dabbing the cardboard with paint, the design is transferred to the cloth.

A stenciled design of a celestial cherub (LEFT) enlivens a plain unlined Roman shade.

PROJECT
Stenciled Cloud Shades

Yellow cherubs lying across puffy yellow clouds use an unlined Roman shade as their canvas. Stenciled in fabric paint of just one color – matched to the border of the fabric – the cherubs lie along the horizontal dowels of the shade.

The stencil can be made by any of the methods described below. To make sure that the cherubs are in line with the dowel pockets, make up the shade (see page 146) and stencil the design before inserting the dowels.

MATERIALS
Fabric
Fabric paints
Stencil cardboard or
*   equivalent*
Cutting mat or
*   equivalent (if cutting*
*   your own stencil)*
Masking tape
Carbon paper

TOOLS
Stencil brush
Ruler
Tape measure
Carpenter's square
Craft knife
Palette knife
Dishes for mixing colors
Clamps or covered
*   bricks*

TECHNIQUE
Preparation
1. Cover your worktable, and if you are cutting your own stencil, use a cutting mat or other dense surface for this.
2. Wash and iron the fabric before the paint is applied. Have some spare fabric on hand for trying out designs and techniques.

Making your own stencil
Stencil shapes can be cut from three different materials:
1. Stencil cardboard: This is made from oiled manila. Draw the stencil onto it and cut out.
2. Acetate: Draw the stencil shape onto this transparent sheet in permanent ink with a technical drawing pen and then cut out. If using several stencils, lay one on top of another in order to show the final design.
3. Untreated cardboard or paper: Waterproof paper or thin cardboard with wax or linseed oil. Paint thicker cardboard with vegetable or linseed oil. This is useful if the design is from a photocopy.

Drawing the stencil
1. If using a stencil or other cardboard, trace the design straight onto tracing paper.
2. Lay a piece of carbon paper, carbon side down, on the stencil cardboard. Lay the tracing on top and draw around the outline again, transferring the design to the cardboard.
3. If using acetate, lay it on top of the design and trace, using a technical drawing pen and permanent ink.
4. If the design needs enlarging, mark a grid on the original, draw a larger grid on the cardboard or acetate, and copy the design with the aid of the grid.
5. Alternatively, the design can be enlarged on a photocopier and then traced as above.
6. Patterns that were not intended as stencil shapes may fall apart if "bridges" are not introduced to hold the sections together.
7. Leave at least 1–2in (2.5–5cm) around the shape to make the stencil stable.
8. Tape the stencil cardboard or acetate to the cutting mat and carefully cut out the stencil shape. Make sure that the blade of the craft knife is very sharp. Use a fluid motion, and try to avoid stopping and starting.

Registration marks
To align the pattern correctly, mark the position of the stencil cardboard with small crosses across the fabric, preferably in removable chalk.

Paint
1. There are many fabric paints and pens available, so follow the printed instructions carefully.
2. The paint is water-soluble and so can be diluted. Take care not to make the paint too thin, since this can cause the design to "bleed."
3. Instead of buying pre-mixed colors, you can mix your own using a basic range. Each color should be mixed with a palette knife (not the brush) in its own dish. The paint pot should then be closed tightly to avoid evaporation. If the paint dries during work, add a little extra water.
4. Avoid using too much paint since this can also cause bleeding at the edges of the design. Test by pressing the brush down onto a cloth or paper towel – it should be barely damp.
5. Allow each application of paint to dry thoroughly before applying another.

Brush
1. A stencil brush is squat and should be held like a pen, at right angles to the cloth. The paint is then applied in a stabbing, dabbing motion.
2. Do not allow the brush to dry out after use, but quickly wash it in mild soap and water. If it has to be left for a while, remember to wrap it in foil to prevent evaporation.

Stencil Shapes

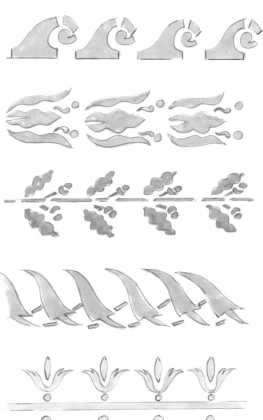

PROJECT
Painted Stripes

One of the quickest and most effective ways of decorating plain cloth is to paint stripes along the surface. Carried out on this scale, it consumes a fair amount of fabric paint, so prepare yourself with plenty of the small pots in which such paint is sold.

Here, a combination of fairly muted colors has been used, but if you prefer a more vivid palette, each stripe could be picked out in a different color against a plain white cotton – sea-greens with blues the color of turquoise, salmon pinks with brilliant oranges.

These stripes are applied using a crumpled rag, made damp (not wet) with fabric paint, giving them an interesting marbled finish. Masking tape gives the stripes a hard edge.

PROJECT
Block-Printed Curtain

Block-printing is one of the simplest ways of decorating cloth. At its most basic, a cut potato can provide a suitable surface for printing. In fact, any raised surface can be dipped in paint and its shape transferred onto cloth by pressure.

Here, a lino cut has been used to create a slightly more difficult two-color teardrop design and border to match the rustic feel of this room. The curtain is held back by an informal reefing system (see page 134).

MATERIALS
Fabric, pre-washed and
  ironed
Two same-size lino
  blocks for the main
  design and two for the
  border
Block-printing ink

TOOLS
Roller
Glass sheet
Chalk
Clamps or covered
  bricks
"V" tool
Gouge

a

TECHNIQUE
1. You will need four lino boards for this design. The two parts of each design (teardrop and border) are printed separately, then superimposed.
2. Cut the boards as follows:
❑ The teardrop shape, with the inner flower shape and the area around the teardrop both cut away (*a*).
❑ The flower shape, with the rest cut away (*b*).
❑ The outer border shape, with the inner shape cut away. The board should be the depth of the border. In this way the edges of

b

c

d

the board produce sharp upper and lower borders (*c*).

❏ The inner border shape, with the outer border cut away (*d*).

3. *a* & *b* & *c* & *d* use same-size lino boards. The designs should be placed in matching positions.

4. The sizes of the board will dictate the pattern repeat. If you want a closely grouped design use a small board and vice versa.

5. First warm the lino board by placing it near a warm oven or the steam from a kettle. This softens the material and makes it easier to work.

6. Mark out the design. Cut around it using the "V" tool, and then cut away the excess using the gouge.

7. Lay the fabric on the worktable and anchor it with clamps or covered bricks.

8. Using chalk, make registration marks to guide the positioning of the lino boards (*e*).

9. Pour a little block-printing ink onto the glass sheet. If necessary, dilute the color with water. Run the roller to and fro to obtain an even coating, and roll it over the lino block.

10. Aligning the corners of the board with the registration marks, press the board firmly down onto the fabric. Repeat the process with each board in turn (*f*).

11. To reuse the boards, wipe them clean with water.

12. Dry the fabric and fix the colors according to the manufacturer's instructions.

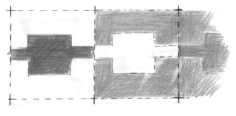

f

e

Finishing Touches

The judicious use of trimmings or decorative details can enhance any curtain, cornice, or shade. Indeed, the plainer the project, the better the end result. A chou or bow might be buried in a busy print, while on plain cream silk or muslin it stands out to great effect. Choux, rosettes, bows, and Maltese crosses are not difficult to make and repay any effort handsomely.

There are also many ways to enhance leading edges. A padded edge gives a luxurious and unusual finish, and a wide band can contrast blocks of color brilliantly. The grander the gesture, the better the effect. Always try to match the scale of the finishing touches to the scale of the project. Big curtains require fat bows and wide edging; small curtains need dainty rosettes and narrow banding.

With bows and Maltese crosses, an additional layer of dressmaker's interfacing or light interlining makes for a fatter, more upholstered finish. If this is desired, imitate the fabric pieces in interfacing, stitch, and turn with the fabric, treating the two layers as one but trimming the seams carefully to avoid any bulk.

Used sparingly and in subtle colors, bows (BELOW) can provide a happy decorative finish in most schemes.

Bows

Bows are among the most traditional of details and have been used for hundreds of years to decorate hats, clothes, and furnishings. Although rooms are often stenciled and chintzes garlanded in a riot of ribbons, bows do not have to be fussy.

Making bows can be almost as simple as tying a shoelace. Make sure that you start with a tube of fabric that is long enough to achieve the right size of bow: it is remarkable how much fabric is needed to achieve one of even modest size. If a hand-tied bow is too bulky in the center, a fake bow is easily made instead. If sewing the tubes that compose fake bows is beyond you, try cutting the fabric into a strip using pinking shears, and take it from there. Perched high on the wall, the bow should not fray to any great extent and the pinking provides additional decoration.

Alternatively, invest in some wide grosgrain ribbon – striped or plain – which will look charming knotted or sewn into a bow.

False Bow

A false bow can be made from three sections: the bow, the central knot, and the sashes.

3. Overlap the raw ends behind and stitch them together (b).

b

MATERIALS
Face fabric
Interfacing (optional)

MAKING UP
Bow
1. Cut a strip of fabric twice the width of the finished bow plus two seam allowances, and twice the depth plus two seam allowances.
2. Fold it in half lengthwise right sides together. Stitch along the long side.
3. Turn and press, with the seam running along the center back.
4. Form into a loop, overlapping raw ends across center back.
5. Make a line of vertical running stitches through the center, passing the needle through to the center front of the loop (a). Pull to form a central gather and secure.

a

Knot
1. Cut a strip of fabric to cover the center of the bow. The strip should be twice the width of the "knot" and long enough to wrap around the center and overlap slightly at the back.
2. Turn in the side edges and wrap around the bow, gathering the strip into loose vertical folds.

Sashes
1. Cut out one long strip with diagonal ends. Fold in half lengthwise, right sides together, and stitch around the sides and one end. Trim, turn, and press.
2. Turn in the open end and slip stitch closed.

c

3. Fold in half and place the folded part over the back of the bow. Stitch into position (c).

Maltese Cross

Maltese crosses sewn to an arrangement of swags, to the overlap of reefed curtains (see page 134), or even across the top of a balloon shade, lend an air of elegance to a window treatment, neither overtly feminine nor excessively fancy. A contrasting edge emphasizes their shape and links them in to the rest of the color scheme.

MATERIALS
Face fabric
Contrasting fabric
Interfacing (optional)

MAKING UP
1. A Maltese cross is made much the same as the main part of a fake bow (see left).
2. Cut the two strips of face fabric that will form the main part of the Maltese cross.
3. Prepare a bias strip in the contrasting fabric (see page 182). Turn in the edges and fold the contrasting strip in half lengthwise, wrong sides together. Press. In this way the stitching line and central fold will be apparent.
4. Stitch, turn, and press the two tubes of fabric. Pin on the bias strip, taking care to align the foldlines (a).
5. Slip stitch (b).

a

6. Form a loop with each section,

b

overlapping at the back. Work a line of gathering stitches up the center of each, through all the layers, and pull up.
7. Place the main sections at right angles to one another and stitch them together at the crossing point (c below).

c

8. Cut a third piece of face fabric. It is made in the same way as the main sections but is a quarter of the size, to cover the central section of the cross. Stitch contrasting banding to the edges in the same way as before, form into a loop (the raw edges overlapping at the back), and stitch the raw edges together.
9. Place at a diagonal on the center of the cross and stitch (d).

d

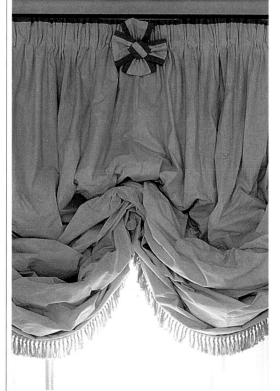

Rosettes

There is something very satisfying about making a rosette, with its fanned pleating and look of precision.

Rosettes are used in much the same way as the previous trimmings. They can be placed where two stationary curtains meet or at the top of a pair of cascades; they can adorn the front of a tieback or run along the top of a shade. By contrast with the other trimmings, however, they rarely need interfacing or interlining – a rosette should not look bulky.

There are two sorts of rosette. The first has crisp folds and forms a circular fan; the second, described below, is a more formal version of the chou, teased out to form regular, fat folds.

MATERIALS
Fabric
Contrasting fabric
Button form

MAKING UP
1. Cut a circle of fabric twice the diameter of the finished rosette plus 1in (2.5cm).
2. Run a line of gathering stitches ½in (12mm) from the edge of the circle (*a*).

3. Draw the thread up tightly to form the center point of the rosette (*b*).

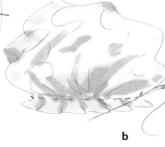

4. Adjust the fanning folds into regular pleats of equal length.
5. Cover the button in contrasting fabric and stitch to the center of the rosette (*c*).

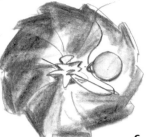

Choux

Unlike the other finishing touches in this section, choux should be kept only for projects on the grand scale. To look right, they need to be a certain size, and are usually the finishing touch to a majestic arrangement of swags. A chou is guaranteed to impress, although the technique is accessible to anyone of average sewing ability.

MATERIALS
Face fabric
Lining
Interlining
Fusible buckram

MAKING UP
1. Cut one circle of fusible buckram and then two circles of interlining to match the finished diameter of the chou.
2. Sandwich the fusible buckram circle between the two pieces of interlining. Then press with a hot iron to fuse the various layers together.
3. Cut another circle in the face fabric, three

times the finished diameter of the chou.
4. Make chalk marks or cut notches to mark quarter sections in the edge of the buckram

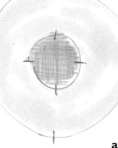

and interlining fabric circles (*a*).
5. Turning the edge of the fabric under that of

the buckram circle, pin the quarter marks of the two pieces together. Then pleat up the rest of the fabric around the circumference of the base. Passing the needle from back to front through all the

layers and close to the edge, stitch the pleats into position (*b* above).

6. Form the balloon of fabric into uneven, random folds and prickstitch them into place (*c*).
7. Cut another circle in lining fabric, so that it is slightly wider than the base. Lay the chou on the lining, turn in the edges and slip stitch into place.

Padded Edge

In the nineteenth and early twentieth century, the trailing hems of heavy velvet curtains would be finished with fat, padded edges. More recently, interior designers have adapted the technique to lend a look of discreet luxury to leading edges. A padded edge is best used on full-length curtains.

MATERIALS
Interlining or batting

MAKING UP
1. The padded edge is formed by a long roll of interlining or batting stitched into the leading edge. The dimensions of the padding depend largely on the scale of the curtain. Allow a large side hem in the curtain to enclose the padding.
2. First experiment with a piece of interlining or batting, rolling it lengthwise to achieve the required circumference.
3. Cut a strip of interlining or batting to the length of the leading edge and to the required width.
4. Roll it up lengthwise to form a long sausage and slip stitch along the raw edge to hold in place – interlining is easier to control than batting (a).

5. With the curtain fabric already locked to the interlining (see page 180) and the heading stiffener in place, position the roll behind the leading edge, from the finished top foldline to the hem fold (b below left).
6. Smooth the side turning over the roll, trapping it with a line of pins.
7. Turn up the hem of the curtain and miter it over the roll. Baste and then prickstitch along the edge of the padding. Match the color of the thread carefully with that of the face fabric. Small stitches will be visible every 1in (2.5cm) (c).

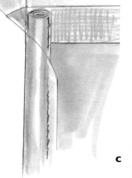

c

8. Lock in the lining across the back of the curtain.
9. Turn in along the edge of the padding and slip stitch into place.

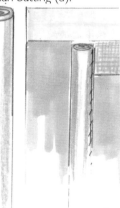

b

a

Contrasting Edge

A generous band of color down the edge of a curtain will enhance the simplest combination of fabrics. Think about the possibilities, say, of edging a simple cream fabric with a wide stripe of dusty pink or midnight blue. Or, in a modern interior, why not juxtapose vivid colors – purples, oranges, and reds – perhaps using whitewashed walls as a foil?

Contrasting bands can be run up the leading edge only, or taken all around the curtain or even the cornice for a more dramatic statement.

MATERIALS
Fabric
Contrasting fabric

MAKING UP
1. The band is treated as an extension of the main fabric.
2. Decide on the width of the band. Cut a strip on the straight grain of the contrasting fabric, twice the width of the finished band plus one seam allowance, and the same length as the finished length plus lower and top hem allowances.

3. With right sides together and raw edges even, stitch the contrasting band to the leading edge of the curtain fabric (a). Press open seam.

4. Continue making up the curtain in the normal way, turning the contrasting edge over the back of the curtain to form the required width (b).

a **b**

Tassel Valance

Many of the most successful decorating projects are based on a high level of improvisation. This is one example. Instead of the usual gathered or stiffened cornice or valance, a strip of lace is combined with an elaborate fringe, looped cord, and tassels, giving a highly original finish to the window. The inspiration came from the mantelpiece of a nineteenth-century parlor. A similar arrangement would have been used to grace the front of a black slate fireplace.

Baroque Embroidered Curtains and Cornice

Swooping baroque curls decorate this cornice and pair of lightweight curtains. The fabric is neither painted nor printed, but embroidered with a technique known as couching. The principle is a simple one: yarn, thin cord, or embroidery floss is laid over the fabric and secured with tiny stitches along its length. This is undeniably time-consuming but, as can be seen, it is well worth the effort.

MATERIALS
Fabric
Embroidery floss, yarn,
* or light cord*

TOOLS
Sharp pencil or chalk
Needle and thread

MAKING UP
1. Use embroidery floss, yarn, or cord that is colorfast and pre-shrunk. Do a test on a small piece if you are in any doubt.
2. Mark out your design on the fabric. Lay the cord along the lines of the design, holding it in place with pins at right angles.
3. Stitch the cord to the cloth with tiny stitches every 1–2in (2.5–5cm), depending on the scale of the design (*a & b*).
4. For quicker results use a zigzag machine-stitch.

a   b

CHAPTER 5

DRILLS AND AWLS, POLES, AND RODS — A KNOWLEDGE
OF THE CORRECT TOOLS AND TECHNIQUES WILL GUIDE
THE CURTAINMAKER THROUGH EVERY PROJECT, FROM
CONCEPTION TO COMPLETION.

fitting

MANY CURTAIN OR SHADE PROJECTS end in failure when measurements are vague or inadequate, the wrong fittings are chosen, or the hanging is incorrect. With a little know-how and effort, however, you can achieve smooth-running, perfect fitting curtains and shades. By checking through the materials required and reading the instructions, you will learn exactly what to ask for and how to use it correctly. Familiarity with the hardware and vocabulary will allow you access to the multitude of options available. Whether you are mounting a brass tieback hook on the wall, measuring for a decorative arrangement of swags, choosing the right rod, or putting up a valance shelf, the detailed instructions in this chapter will put every task within reach.

Curtain tiebacks can be as practical or as imaginative as you wish.
Here, a unique treatment bracelets these curtains of the
richest crimson velvet.

Tools and Accessories

Standing on top of a wobbly chair, inadequate tape measure in hand, reaching for the inaccessible corner of a high window, is an experience guaranteed to put most people off the whole idea of homemade curtains or shades. Starting with the right equipment eases every task and is well worth the initial outlay. Always keep an orderly tool box with a stock of basic materials – staples, screws, and bolts, for example. Careful labeling will also help to speed up operations.

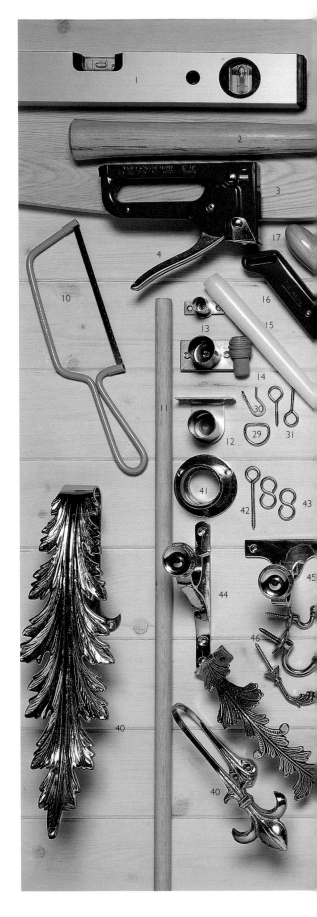

From left to right, top to bottom:

  1. Carpenter's level
  2. Hammer
  3. Curved-fronted valance shelf
  4. Staple gun
  5. Retractable steel tape measure
  6. Cloth clamp
  7. Calculator
  8. Notebook
  9. 12in hard plastic ruler
 10. Hacksaw
 11. Dowel
 12. Top-fixing rod socket
 13. Face-fixing rod socket
 14. Shade pull
 15. Wax candle
 16. Craft knife
 17. Awl
 18. Screwdriver
 19. Eyelet punch and eyelets
 20. Brackets (cornice)
 21. Brackets (shelf)
 22. Plastic plugs and galvanized steel screws
 23. Thread
 24. Tailor's chalk
 25. Seam ripper
 26. Web
 27. Sewing machine needles
 28. Thimble
 29. D-ring
 30. Sew-on hook
 31. Screw eyes

 32. Wallboard bolts
 33. Split rings
 34. Brass rings
 35. Spacer
 36. Clip-on rings
 37. Curtain tapes
 38. Pincushion
 39. Carpenter's square
 40. Holdbacks
 41. Pole socket
 42. Vine eye
 43. S-rings
 44. Pole end bracket
 45. Pole support bracket
 46. Tieback hooks
 47. Holdbacks
 48. Rings (gilded, plain wood)
 49. Lead weights
 50. Shade cord
 51. Piping cord
 52. Roller shade cord fixing
 53. Coat hook
 54. Awning cleat
 55. Scissors
 56. Pinking shears
 57. Pin-on hook
 58. Brass hooks
 59. Plastic hooks
 60. Pleater hook
 61. Hook-and-loop tape
 62. Covered chain weights
 63. Iron

Fitting Poles, Valance Shelves, and Rods

Curtains and shades can be hung from any number of fittings, from the simplest wooden pole to elaborate patented multi-rod arrangements in aluminum. The main options to consider before making your choice are practical and aesthetic. Aim for a system that will operate efficiently while complementing the style of your curtains, drapes, or shades. Try to use the best quality rod that you can afford – it will pay in the long run – and take special care to mount it securely. If you are in any doubt, go back to your supplier and ask for advice.

POLE
(below left)
❑ If the curtains or drapes are to be drawn back, a pole is the most attractive solution and does not block the light.
❑ Poles are unsuitable for shades, cornices, and valances, although you can have the best of both worlds with an attached valance (see page 118) or a draped pole backed with curtains on a hidden rod.
❑ Finials and rings provide additional decoration.
❑ Poles are impractical on bow windows.
❑ Bay windows can be fitted with poles but these must be held by special brackets at the angles of the window, so the curtains cannot draw all the way around – each section of window carries its own pair of curtains (thereby reducing incoming light). A false pole (see page 171) is another way of using a pole at a bay window.

VALANCE SHELF
(*a* below)
❑ A valance shelf is a wood board, mounted above the window on brackets. A cornice, valance, swag, Roman shade, balloon shade, or stationary curtains can be hung from it, and the base can be fitted with a shade mounting board or a curtain rod.
❑ A valance shelf is essential for multiple layers – a cornice with a Roman shade behind it or a valance with a pair of curtains, for example.
❑ When a pair of curtains hangs alone, you can choose between a pole, an exposed rod and a covered cornice board.
❑ Do not be confused by the plethora of high-tech, multi-rod systems, often custom-made. These can be expensive and are often no more effective than a simple board, fitted with the appropriate rods or shade brackets.

a

COVERED CORNICE BOARD
(b & c below)
❏ A wood valance shelf, covered with fabric or painted and fitted with a curtain rod, is known as a covered cornice board. A 2in (5cm) band of buckram or plywood, covered with the curtain fabric, is attached to the front of the shelf to hide the rod. The curtain hooks extend just below the cornice board while the top edge of the curtain runs along the front, hiding the cornice board when the curtains are closed. This is a useful way to disguise the rod when there is no valance. The advantages of a covered cornice board are similar to those of a pole – no loss of light, and the decorative possibilities of an exposed heading.
❏ Use when a pole is less practical.

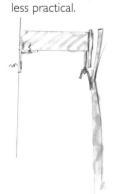

b

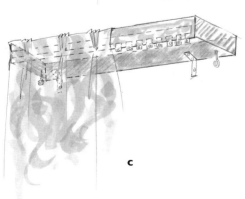

c

Mounting

Before you begin, examine the wall, window frame, or ceiling surface, and check that you have all the right tools. Ask someone to help, since working on your own can be tricky. Windows and floors may not be level, but unless they are wildly off kilter, place fittings parallel to windows, without using a carpenter's level. Only roller shades need perfectly level fittings. It is often impossible to know what lies behind a plaster surface, so mount rods, poles, valance shelves, and boards with caution. Drill a small exploratory hole to test the depth of the plaster and to see what lies behind it. Then take appropriate action.

WALL AND CEILING SURFACES
Plaster
❏ Most walls, unless of bare concrete, are covered with a layer of plaster of varying thickness.
❏ If the fittings are not destined to take too much weight – for example, a light rod or tieback hook – inserting plastic plugs into the plaster should be adequate.
❏ Heavy drapes or shades need deeper mountings into the surface behind the plaster.

Wood
To avoid splits, drill pilot holes with the appropriate drill bit or pierce with an awl, then put in the screw.
❏ Avoid inserting screws close to the edge of the wood, since this may cause it to split.

Concrete
❏ Some windows have concrete lintels, and modern buildings often have concrete ceilings. This is a hard surface to drill, but will provide a firm base.
❏ A hammer-action drill is necessary for drilling into concrete. A pneumatic hammer-action drill is even more effective.
❏ Use masonry bolts with the appropriate plastic plugs.

Steel
❏ Steel lintels are sometimes found over windows: the hollow sound of a drill on steel is easily recognizable.
❏ Sometimes the plaster in front may be deep enough to take the fixing. Otherwise use self-drilling screws called drivers, or change to a drill bit appropriate for metal.

❏ If the screws cannot be screwed directly into the metal, drill a slightly larger hole and insert plastic plugs.
❏ Do not drill into a steel lintel from below. Move the fitting clear of the lintel, or bring the fitting forward on brackets.

Brick
❏ Use a carbide drill bit and masonry bolts with plastic plugs. Bolts 2in (5cm) in size are usually strong enough, but you may need twice the length and heavyduty plugs if the brick has softened with age.

Thermal (breeze) blocks
❏ Plastic plugs and 2in (50mm) holes will anchor most fittings into thermal blocks.
❏ Do not use a hammer-action drill, since thermal blocks are soft and need gentle handling. A masonry drill bit is better.
❏ Leave a gap of at least 2in (5cm) between the edge of the recess and the drill hole.
❏ Specially ribbed plugs for thermal blocks are available.

Wood-frame walls
❏ Wood-frame walls are constructed of wallboard nailed to wooden studs. Studs run up both sides of the window, and a wooden lintel, or "header," goes across the top.
❏ Fixings should be screwed through the wallboard into the studs or header.

❏ You will need expansion bolts or toggle bolts between the studs. Wall plugs are unsuitable.

Ceilings
❏ Ceiling joists run at right angles to floorboards. To identify their exact position, check the floor above and then run a line of exploratory holes into the ceiling; these can then be filled in afterward. Screws 2in (5cm) in size will hold most fittings.
❏ Concrete: Proceed as for concrete walls.
❏ Wallboard: Use expansion or toggle bolts or screw into the joists.
❏ Lath and plaster: For light curtains, screw into the laths. Try to avoid over-tightening the screws since this may split the laths. Otherwise, screw into the joists.

WIRING
❏ Before starting work, locate any wiring in the room. Drilling into wires is extremely dangerous.
❏ Electrical wires run directly up or down from a switch or socket. If necessary, you can discover the direction by unscrewing the front plate.

PIPES
❏ Take care, too, to avoid pipes when drilling into ceilings or around windows.
❏ A range of simple gadgetry is available for locating pipes, wires, and joists.

Poles

A selection of gilded finials (BELOW) – pineapples, arrowheads, and feathers – of a type available from a variety of sources. Their deliberately antiqued gilding makes an exquisite contrast to the deep folds of a dark velvet or silk curtain.

Acurtain without a cornice or valance can look starkly utilitarian, but a handsome pole can provide a decorative lift. As well as being functional, poles lend distinctive style. They range from contemporary wrought iron finished in a shepherd's crook or curl, through shades of stained and varnished wood, to thick reeded brass poles and thin brass rods. Every sort of antique model has been sought out and copied: gilded rams' heads, acanthus leaves, painted pineapples, and scores of brass arrowheads. There are also some interesting modern designs.

Among the chief charms of the curtain pole is versatility. Apart from holding a simple pair of curtains, poles can also be swathed in swags or encased by a rod-pocket or a poufed heading. In fact, poles are hard to beat for showing off a heading, perhaps corded or decorated with choux or Maltese crosses. Always be prepared to invest in the best pole you can afford. It is worth remembering that a highly inexpensive fabric will often appear the ultimate in luxury when set against a pair of grand gilded finials and a fat mahogany-stained pole.

POLES

❑ Brass or wood poles come in various diameters, from 1in (2.5cm) to 3in (8cm).

❑ Wood dowels are available from lumberyards and craft stores. Less substantial than real curtain poles, they are up to 1½in (4cm) in diameter and are used for hanging light curtains and sheers. A dowel is generally mounted using rod sockets, while curtain poles are mounted with brackets or pole sockets.

❑ You can hang wood, brass or, clip-on rings on a pole or dowel.

❑ Clip-on rings act like a set of clothespins and can be attached to simple squares of cloth – Indian saris or checked tablecloths – for easy, improvised curtains and valances (see below).

❑ Tied, tab, or rod-pocket curtains will go over the pole without the need for rings.

BRACKETS AND SOCKETS

❑ Poles rest on brackets fixed to the wall on each side of the window.

❑ The brackets can either come flush against the edge of the finial (useful for rod-pocket headings, which are impeded by a bracket) or, more usually, they are positioned several inches in from the edge of the finial, with one or more rings left outside the bracket.

❑ If one or both ends of the pole is up against a wall or the window frame with no room for a finial, the pole can be slotted into a pole socket.

❑ Brass or chrome-plated rod sockets are best if glass curtains or other lightweight curtains are to hang from a dowel.

❑ Poles can be bought with all the parts pre-packed, but finials, brackets, and rings, as well as the poles themselves, can also be bought separately.

❑ When purchasing items individually, remember to make sure that finials, rings, and brackets fit the pole or dowel.

FALSE POLES

❑ Conventional curtain poles are not always suitable for bay and bow windows so false poles, or decorative traverse rods, come into use. These give the appearance of a pole, seeming to turn the angles of the window, but a hidden rod, set into the base, carries the hooks.

❑ Decorative traverse rods use overclip brackets that allow the curtains to pass below.

Draping a pole in a length of fabric (ABOVE) is a quick way to create an elaborate effect. The curtains hang not from the pole but from a hidden rod.

An antique pole, brass rings, and heavy gold tassels on knotted ropes add an elegant effect to these unpleated curtains (ABOVE).

FINISHES
❏ Pre-packed poles come with an existing finish, but unfinished wooden poles can be stained, painted, or otherwise treated.

❏ It is a good idea to run a candle or silicone spray along the top of the pole and inside the rings to make the curtains run smoothly.

Brass poles
❏ Brass poles are usually finished with a clear varnish that will resist tarnishing. The varnish can sometimes be stripped to give an antiqued effect. Before doing this, check the type of varnish, and consult an art supply store for advice.

Wrought-iron poles
❏ Wrought-iron poles give any room an up-to-date air, marrying well with colorful cotton checks and stripes, or bold designs in linen. The scope for twisting and turning each end is infinite – corkscrews or curls are just two of the more popular shapes.

Wood poles
❏ Paint or stain and varnish can be applied to untreated wood poles and rings.

❏ Apply stain thinly, wiping off any residue. Build up a number of layers, depending on the depth of color required, and finish with a coat of varnish. Let dry thoroughly.

❏ Oil-based eggshell-finish paint is best for painting poles.

❏ Build up the paint in thin layers, allowing each to dry thoroughly.

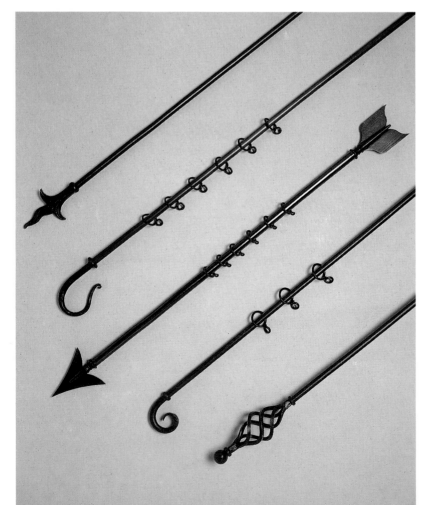

LEFT ABOVE (from top to bottom):
1. Brass rod with fleur-de-lys finial
2. Brass twisted pole with acanthus finial
3. Polished steel pole with copper lily finial
4. Steel rod with tassel finial
5. Steel rod with corkscrew finial
6. Polished steel rod with glass finial

LEFT BELOW (from top to bottom):
1. Steel pole with fleur-de-lys finial
2. Steel pole with shepherd's crook finial
3. Steel pole with arrow finial
4. Wrought-iron pole with ram's horn finial
5. Wrought-iron pole with basketwork finial

RIGHT ABOVE (from top to bottom):
1. Reeded mahogany pole with ram's head finial
2. Ebony pole with cherrywood finial
3. Wood pole with gilded heraldic finial
4. Stained wood pole with domed finial
5. Wood pole with gilded flame finial
6. Reeded gilt pole with pineapple finial

RIGHT BELOW (from top to bottom):
1. Wood pole with pewter finish and spearhead finial
2. Natural ash pole with pyramid finial
3. Natural beech pole with ball finial
4. Stained wood pole with pineapple finial
5. Wood pole with dome finial
6. Stained wood pole with seahorse finial

Dormer window or doorway rods
❑ Both types of rods swing out from the wall. A hinged dormer rod is a swing-arm that swings back to the side wall for a deeply recessed window. A doorway rod moves back with the door as it opens.

MOUNTING POLES
❑ When mounting a curtain pole, bear in mind that the curtains will hang from the rings, with the top edge of each curtain running about an inch (a few centimeters) below the pole. Place the pole high enough to stop light coming over the top of the curtains, i.e. slightly higher than a valance shelf.
❑ Often the brackets will not project the pole clear of the window trim. If so, fit the brackets onto blocks of wood screwed into the wall. The blocks can be

a

painted or covered in wallpaper or fabric (a).
❑ Support the center of long poles with a support bracket. As a rough guide, a 1in (2.5cm) pole carrying heavy curtains or drapes will need a support bracket if it is

over 5ft (1.5m) in length, as will a 1½in (4cm) pole if over 6ft (1.8m) or a 2in (5cm) pole if over 7ft (2.1m).

Rod-pocket headings
Rod-pocket curtains are stationary – i.e. the headings are never drawn back. A pocket in the top is gathered onto a pole. There are four options:
1. Slot the curtains onto the pole, mark the positions of the brackets, and make two small holes in the back of the pockets. The brackets can then pierce the pockets (b).

b

2. If no finials are attached to the ends of the pole, slip stitch the ends of the pocket and tack to the end surfaces of the pole.
3. Use rod sockets (for thin poles/dowels) which, once in place, are covered by the ends of the pocket. A pole socket will act in the same way for curtains hung inside a window recess or inside two projecting wall surfaces.
4. Place the brackets flush with the insides of the finials and overlap with pocket edges.

Rods

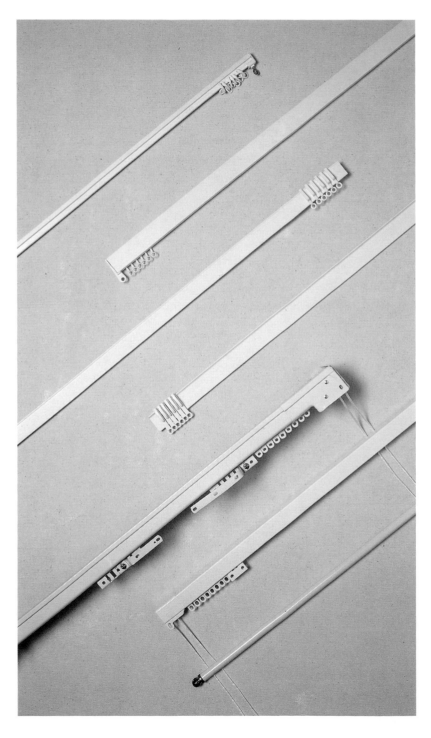

A rod that slides cleanly, with properly adjusted cords, firmly mounted on the wall, will fully repay the investment of time and money. Numerous rods and systems are available; they can be motorized or manual, single or multiple, plastic or metal, traverse or flat, bent or straight. Ask the supplier's advice and consult the instructions carefully.

Basically, the choice is between a traverse rod or a flat curtain rod. A traverse rod has a loop of cord on one side, held taut by a tension pulley. Pulling the cord moves little slides along the rod; the curtain hooks are attached to the slides so that the curtains open and close, preventing the leading edges from wearing out or getting grubby.

A two-way traverse rod moves two panels at once in opposite directions. The leading edges overlap, minimizing light penetration and cold drafts. A one-way traverse rod opens and closes a single curtain.

A flat track, either metal or plastic, lacks such sophistications. With it, curtains are opened by hand. However, it is easy to cut down and to fit, and so is ideal for simple projects and the inexperienced curtain hanger.

Always choose a rod that will support the weight of the curtains or drapes, and make sure that it is securely mounted.

LEFT (from top to bottom):
1–4. Lightweight flat plastic rods
5. Two-way metal traverse rod
6. Plastic traverse rod
7. Sash rod for lightweight curtains and sheers

RODS
Flat
❑ These rods may be plastic or aluminum. They are designed for sheers and for lightweight curtains.

Traverse
❑ These rods are suitable for most curtains and drapes. The easiest to mount are telescopic steel tracks, the length of which is adjustable. Otherwise, use a hacksaw to cut the rod to length. Do not allow the cords to twist.

❑ The cords can be held separate and tight around a tension pulley screwed to the baseboard. Alternatively, cut the looped cord and slot each pulley cord through a brass pull. The effect will be decorative, but the cords are more likely to twist.

❑ Traverse rods are designed for two curtains to be drawn back to either side, but it is possible to buy one-way traverse rods to move only one panel in one direction.

Sash rods
❑ Round sash rods with small brackets that are either separate or built into the ends are useful for sheer curtains. A tension rod has a spring-tension mechanism to hold it within the window frame so that brackets are not necessary.

Bay windows
❑ Ideally rods around bay windows should be suspended from a custom-made valance shelf, which has been measured and fitted professionally. Problems can arise when flexible rods are bent around tight corners, since the curtains may not open and close smoothly.

Bow windows
❑ Mounting valance shelves into the curve of a bow window is even more difficult than for a bay window and an exposed, plastic rod often tends to spoil the effect.

FITTING RODS AND VALANCE SHELVES
❑ As a general rule, a shelf carrying a single rod should be 5in (12.5cm) deep, while a shelf for a double rod should measure at least 7in (18cm).

❑ To give the appearance of extra width to a narrow window, extend the valance shelf or exposed rod at least 4in (10cm) to each side of the window.

❑ Paint the valance shelf to match the wall or fabric, or staple curtain or shade fabric to the board, wrapping it like a package.

❑ Attach the brackets to the wall about 4in (10cm) above the window. If you want to make the window appear taller, place the brackets nearer the ceiling. Screw the shelf to the brackets.

❑ Stationary curtains, with a generous overlap, will disguise a high valance shelf, or a cornice can be used to cover the space between shelf and window. Try not to expose any wall space above the window.

❑ Screw the rod to the base of the board. Leave a 1in (2.5cm) gap between the end of the rod and the edge of the board.

❑ The track should be suspended at least 2¾in (7cm) behind the front edge of the shelf. For use with covered cornice boards, the rod should be behind the back of the buckram or the plywood band.

❑ Insert a vine eye (a screw eye on a longer stem) into each rear corner of the base of the shelf to hold the curtain returns in place. The outer left- and right-hand hooks in the curtain headings will be slotted into the vine eyes, holding the outer edges of the curtains flush with the wall.

Multiple rods
❑ When more than one rod is needed, the front rod should hang from a valance shelf. The second will either hang behind it from the same shelf, or be attached to the window trim or wall above the window.

❑ The second rod should be placed at least 2in (5cm) behind the first and, if hanging from the same board, at least 1½in (4cm) from the wall.

Cornices, valances, and covered cornice boards
❑ The front edge of the wood valance shelf carries either a cornice, a valance, or a 2in (5cm) band of buckram or plywood covered in fabric (known as a covered cornice board) to hide the rod. The rod lies directly behind the cornice board.

❑ To fit a valance shelf into a bay window, make a paper pattern of the window angles. Cut the three pieces of wood to length, angle the ends to fit snugly against one another, and fix the three sections using mending plates and screws (a below).

❑ Curve-fronted or D-shaped valance shelves are most attractive for stationary curtains, cornices, or valances. In the latter case a curtain rod, fixed to the base of the shelf, can be bent slightly to follow the curve (b). Be sure that they do not finish at too sharp an angle because this may well cause problems with any rod running below and in positioning the brackets.

Brackets
❑ It is very important to use strong brackets to hold the valance shelf because regular right-angled brackets may bend under the strain. Special brackets, designed for use with curtains and shades, are available.

❑ Reinforced shelf brackets are strong enough but have a rib that impedes the action of the hooks along the rod. With these you will have to use a washer-like spacer to lower the rod slightly, clear of the rib (c & d).

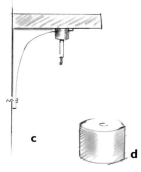

c

d

b

a

Fitting Shades and Reefed Curtains

Similar methods are used for fitting shades or reefed curtains. First fix a valance shelf above the window using strong brackets. The depth of the shelf will be dictated by a windowsill that might interfere with the back of the shade or curtain and by the depth of the window trim. The shade should hang as close to the window as possible but there should be sufficient room for the screw eyes in the base of the shelf to operate effectively. Bear in mind that the ends of the shelf can be hidden by the returns of stationary curtains, a cornice, valance, or balloon shade but not by a Roman shade.

ROMAN AND BALLOON SHADES
See pages 146–150.
1. Staple hook-and-loop tape along the top of the shelf just behind the front edge (Roman shades) or to the front edge and the ends of the shelf (balloon shades).
2. Position a screw eye in the base of the slat, above each line of rings on the back of the shade. Position another toward the end of the slat to carry the cord to the end of the shelf on the pull-up side (Roman or balloon shades).
3. Insert an awning cleat or pair of knobs into the wall between chest and waist height, below the point at which the pull cord

emerges. These hold the cord while the shade is raised (shades).
4. If a Roman or balloon shade is to hang behind a pair of conventional curtains, screw a 1¼in (3cm) square batten to the base of the valance shelf, at least 2in (5cm) behind the front rod and at least 1½in (4cm) away from the wall. Insert screw eyes in the base of the batten for the shade's cording to run through.

ROLLER SHADES
See page 143.
❑ Roller shades are held in special brackets, either inside the window opening or outside it on the wood trim.
❑ You will need a carpenter's level to align the brackets.
❑ If hanging inside the opening, make sure that imperfectly straight walls do not interfere with the edges of the shade.
❑ Roller shades are operated either by a side-winding mechanism or by a spring roller.

Undertensioned roller shades:
1. Roll the shade down.
2. Take the shade out of the brackets.
3. Roll it up by hand.
4. Replace the roller in the brackets.
5. Pull the shade down.
6. Repeat if necessary. Because the spring is self-winding, the tension will build up.
7. Be careful not to over-wind because this will immobilize the shade completely.

REEFING
See page 134.
Reefing is based on much the same principle as the balloon shade, using a valance shelf fitted with screw eyes to carry the cording.
❑ A screw eye should be fitted to the wall or wood trim around the window directly below each outer screw eye on either side, behind the curtain's outer edges. These will guide the diagonal cord up the back of the curtain into a vertical line up to the base of the valance shelf.

Hanging Curtains and Shades

Hanging curtains or shades can be a very stressful operation and is not to be undertaken lightly. Interlined curtains can be very heavy and Roman or balloon shades unwieldy so enlist help to hold the stepladder and bear some of the weight as you slot the hooks or match the lines of hook-and-loop tape. Prepare as much as possible in advance – forward planning will save time in the long run.

Training Curtains

Curtains must be "trained" if folds are to form whenever they are in use.

1. With the curtains open, tease the folds into place. Draw the curtains, retaining the folds (*a*).

2. Starting from just above the hem, tie the strips of lining or interlining around each curtain at 12in (30cm) intervals to hold the folds in place. Take special care not to crush the fabric (*b* right).

3. Leave the curtains to hang for four to seven days.

4. Once the folds are set, all layers will move as one.

Points to remember

❑ Always protect curtains and shades with plastic tubing while in transit. Wear gloves to avoid marking curtains or shades.

❑ Pull up the cord in the curtain tape evenly to the exact finished width before hanging. Insert the correct number of hooks. If the curtain is very wide, mark the tape into sections and pull it up in stages.

❑ Never cut the curtain tape cords.

❑ While hooking a curtain onto a track, support the weight by carrying the curtain thrown over one shoulder.

❑ Avoid working with your arms above your head; this will quickly exhaust you or make you dizzy.

❑ Start to hang the curtains from the center – the weight is then distributed more evenly and later adjustments are easier. Do not begin by hooking the curtain to the overlap arms; it will bend under the weight.

❑ Don't try to iron curtains and shades once they are in place.

❑ When fitting a swag or a heavy cornice, use finishing nails. To hide the nail, work the head behind the front layer of fabric.

Sewing Techniques

sing the correct stitches and sewing techniques is the key to making successful curtains or shades. The layers should hang together as if attached by an invisible force. There should be no signs of internal tensions where stitches are too tight; nor should the lining or interlining sag. Carefully clipped seams, neatly mitered corners, and accurately matched patterns all contribute to curtains, cornices, or shades that hang well and will last a lifetime.

Cutting Out

Accurate cutting is a very important part of curtainmaking. Always check your measurements before you begin and use a large, sharp pair of scissors.

Finding the fabric grain

❏ Most fabrics should be cut on the straight grain (unless, like swags, welting, and contrasting edging, they are deliberately cut on the cross grain).

❏ To find the straight grain on woven fabrics, pull a weft (horizontal) thread.

❏ Snip across the selvage edge close to the end of the fabric and ease out one thread from across the fabric with a pin. Then cut along the channel formed by the withdrawn thread.

❏ Patterns are not always printed on the straight grain. When the pattern has been printed slightly off-grain, cut out following the pattern, not the grain. Patterned fabric can be cut out up to 2in (5cm) out of alignment.

❏ When cutting fabric lengths, snip off a corner at the top of each length. In this way it will always be evident which way the fabric should be joined, so any pile or shading will run in the same direction.

Sewing

❏ Use short lengths of thread (except for lockstitch) – long ones will snag and knot.

❏ Work with a single thread. For greater strength use a stronger thread.

❏ Secure the stitches firmly at each end.

❏ Wear a comfortable thimble for all hand sewing.

❏ Make sure that the stitch is neither too tight nor too loose.

❏ Seam allowance is always ⅝in (15mm), unless otherwise stated.

Hand Stitches

The following hand stitches are those most commonly used for sewing for the home. The sizes of stitches given in the instructions are for guidance only. Larger-scale projects can use proportionately larger stitches.

Backstitch

Backstitch imitates machine stitching and is the strongest hand stitch. It will hold two fabric pieces firmly together.

1. Bring the needle through to the upper side of the fabric.

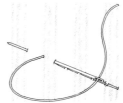

2. Insert the needle ¼ in (6mm) behind where the thread emerges, bringing it out the same distance in front.

3. Continue to the end. Stitches underneath will be twice as long.

Blind-catchstitch

This stitch holds hems on heavier curtains, when it is often worked over a raw edge. Blind-catchstitch is also used to join together lengths of interlining and batting, and to attach non-fusible buckram.

1. Work from left to right, with the needle pointing left.

2. Pick up a few threads in the curtain, then, working diagonally, take a small stitch in from the hem edge, with the needle still pointing left.

3. Continue, forming diagonal crossing stitches.

4. To join batting, place two pieces with edges butting together but not overlapping, and blind-catchstitch across where they meet.

5. Blind-catchstitch can be used to join overlapping widths of interlining in the same way.

6. A blind-catchstitch is used to secure non-fusible buckram to the face fabric or interlining.

Ladderstitch

This form of basting allows a pattern to be matched accurately before the seam is stitched. The sewing is done from the right side (front) of the fabric.

1. Turn under and press one seam allowance on the first piece of fabric.

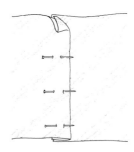

2. With right sides up, overlap the first piece and the second piece. Maneuver the pieces so that the pattern matches horizontally.

3. With a knotted thread starting under the fold, take equal, alternating stitches down through the fold and then just to one side of it, forming tiny, horizontal "ladder" stitches across the join.

4. When the ladder-stitching is complete, you can fold the fabric pieces right sides together and stitch the seam in the usual way.

Lockstitch

This stitch is used for linking interlining to the main fabric, and lining to the interlining, so that all layers will move as one. Use a thread that exactly matches the fabric, and position vertical lines of lockstitching every half fabric width for the interlining and every fabric width for the lining.

1. Place the fabric right side down. Position the interlining over the wrong side of the fabric and smooth the interlining flat.

2. Turn the interlining back on itself to form a vertical fold up the center of the first width.

3. With the thread secured to the interlining back, pass the needle through the interlining fold close to the edge, then pick up a few threads of fabric.

4. Do not pull the stitch tight, but leave a loop. Pass the needle through the loop and take a second stitch, 4–6in (10–15cm) below the first.

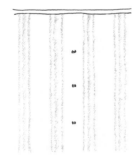

5. Use the same technique to lock the lining to the back of the curtain, folding the lining back over the interlining.

6. Unlike other techniques, lockstitch requires long lengths of thread to avoid the tension created by a line of stitches.

Overcasting

This stitch finishes the raw fabric edge by hand.

1. Secure the knotted thread on the wrong side.

2. Working from right to left, take the thread diagonally over the raw edge, placing stitches

about ¼–½in (6–12mm) down from the raw edge. Do not pull the stitches too tight.

3. Use deeper stitches on fabrics that ravel.

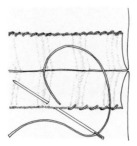

Prickstitch

This is a strong stitch, like backstitch, but is less visible.

1. Work from the right side of the fabric and from right to left.

2. Fasten the thread on the wrong side and pass the needle vertically through the fabric.

3. Make a small reverse stitch, then bring the needle to the right side ½in (12mm).

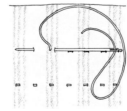

4. Small stitches show on the right side, with long, overlapping ones on the wrong side.

Running stitch

This stitch is used to gather fabric by hand.

1. Begin with a small backstitch to hold the line of stitching in place; then work in and out of the fabric, making even stitches and spaces. The size of the stitches depends on the fullness of gathering required. Use a single thread and

leave a generous length of thread unsecured at the end.

2. Work a second line of identical running stitches above the first, starting from the same side. Match the stitch positions in the two lines precisely and check that the stitching lines are parallel. Leave the end of the second thread unsecured.

3. To gather, draw up the loose ends together to form evenly spaced gathers.

4. To hold the gathers in place, wrap the threads together in a figure-eight around a pin placed vertically through the fabric at the end of the stitching.

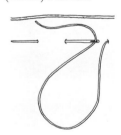

5. On very long lengths of gathering, divide the fabric into equal sections and gather separately.

Slip stitch

Use this stitch for hems on lightweight fabrics and for holding down seam allowances.

1. Work with a long, fine needle, almost parallel to the stitching line, from right to left.

2. Pick up a few threads of the flat fabric, then pass the needle through the folded hem, close to the edge. It is important to pick up only the minimum number of threads with each stitch.

3. Pull the stitch firm, but not tight.

Basting

Basting will hold two pieces of fabric together temporarily.

1. Secure the thread with a knot on the wrong side.

2. Working from the right side, just inside the seamline, pass the needle in and out through all the layers at approximately ¾in (19mm) intervals.

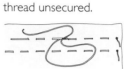

3. Try to avoid stitching over basting; caught threads are difficult to remove.

Seams

When choosing the correct seam for your project, take into account the weight of the fabric and the position of the seam.

Plain seam

This is the seam to use when joining any two pieces of fabric.

1. With right sides together, raw edges even, sew a line of basting stitches just outside the seamline. Stitch ⅝in (15mm) in from the raw edge.

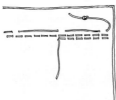

2. Work a few stitches in reverse at each end of the seam to prevent it from separating. Remove the basting stitches. Press open.

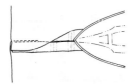

3. To avoid having to baste, pin seams at right angles to seamline. Stitch, using chalk line as a guide. (Stitch slowly over the pins.)

Square corners

To avoid bulk, cut diagonally across corners, close to the stitches.

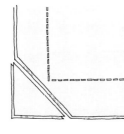

Acute-angle corners

1. Work a few stitches across the corner.
2. If necessary, reinforce with reverse stitching.

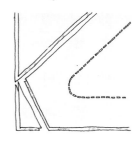

3. Cut the seam allowance across the corner, trimming until all bulk is removed.

Clipping straight seams

1. To ease tight selvages, cut into the seam allowance at 2in (5cm) intervals. The cut is diagonal to the seamline.

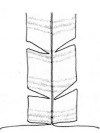

2. Avoid clipping if there is light behind the curtain or shade so that the seam shows through to the right side. Trim the selvages generously.

Clipping curved seams

1. Clip notches into the seam allowance at right angles to seamline on inner curves.

2. On outward curves, cut out notches at right angles to the seamline.
3. Tight bends will require closer spaced clipping.

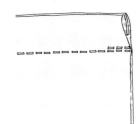

Finishing raw edges

If a raw edge is visible or likely to fray, use zigzag stitch worked ¼in (6mm) in from the raw edge.

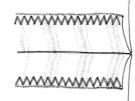

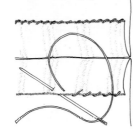

French seam

If a seam is visible from the back or tends to fray badly, use a French seam. This works for lightweight fabrics only.

1. Stitch a ⅜in (1cm) plain seam (see above), with wrong sides together.

2. Press open and trim the seam allowance to half its original width.
3. Turn wrong side out.
4. Stitch a plain ¼in (6mm) seam, being careful to encase the raw edges completely.

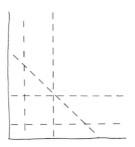

Flat-fell seam

This self-neatening seam is stronger than a French seam.

1. With right sides together, stitch a plain seam.
2. Press both seam allowances to one side of the seamline.
3. Trim the lower seam allowance to half the original width.

4. Fold the edge of the upper seam allowance over the raw edge of the lower. Pin at right angles to the seam.
5. Stitch down the seam again just inside the folded edge.

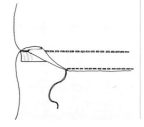

Hems

Mitered corners

Miters make for crisp corners and help to remove bulk.

1. Turn in the side hem, then the lower hem, and press. Open out again.

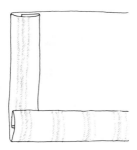

2. Turn the triangular corner over, using the finished corner point of the fabric as the pivot, matching the foldlines.

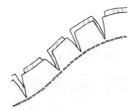

3. Turn up the single or double lower hem and side hem to form the miter. Slip stitch.

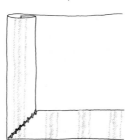

4. If the mitered corner remains bulky, trim excess fabric but follow the same instructions. Trim excess interlining if necessary, unless you are ever likely to let the hem down again.

Machine-stitched miters

These are suitable for a single hem in lightweight fabric.

1. To machine stitch a mitered corner, fold the fabric at the corner, matching selvages.

2. From the corner point, run a line of stitching at right angles

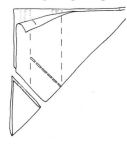

to the fold. Trim close to the seamline.

3. Turn out the corner and press open.

Decorative Trimming

Edges can be trimmed with welting, ruffles, fringe, braid, or ribbon.

Cutting a bias strip

Bias strips are used for contrasting edging or for piping.

1. Cut off one corner along the bias. Mark the fabric with parallel cutting lines from this edge. Use yardstick edges as a guide.

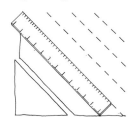

2. When joining two bias strips together, follow the straight grain. With right sides together, match the diagonal seamlines, slightly overlapping the raw edges, and stitch. Press open.

Cutting a continuous bias strip

1. To cut a continuous length, first cut out a rectangle of fabric with a length that is more than twice the width.

2. Fold the fabric diagonally from the top corner so that the cut edge lies along the selvage edge. Press along the fold.

3. Unfold and cut along the creased line. Stitch the triangle to the opposite end.

4. Mark off the strip width in chalk lines parallel to the cut ends.

5. Mark a ¼ in (6mm) seam allowance down both side edges.

6. Mark points A and B on the seamline – A is two strips down, B is one strip down.

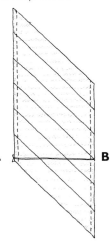

7. Fold the fabric with right sides together, matching A and B together. Stitch down the marked seamline. Press open.

8. Cut around the spiral, beginning with the overlapping end at the top and following the marked lines.

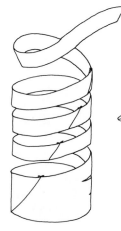

Piping

Piping cord should be pre-shrunk and suitably sized for the scale of the project.

1. Measure the edge, allowing extra for the corners and for joining.

2. To calculate the width of encasing fabric strips, allow the circumference of the piping cord plus twice the seam allowance.

3. Cut strips on the bias and join them together until they are the same length as the cord. Press the seams open.

4. Place the cord on the wrong side of the strip. Fold the strip in half, enclosing cord and matching raw edges.

5. Baste and stitch close to the edge of the piping cord, using the zipper foot on the machine.

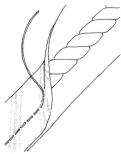

Joining piping

1. To join two ends of piping, cut the fabric and cord to length, allowing ½ in (12mm) for the overlap. Fold in one raw edge. The edges are diagonal, following the cross grain.

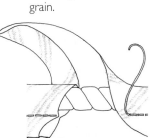

2. Undo the ends of the cord and twist loosely together. Wind sewing thread around the splice to hold. Overlap the folded and raw edges. Using tiny stitches, join the two ends of casing. To finish the raw end of the welting, trim and turn the casing's edge to the inside. Slip stitch the edges together, encasing the cord.

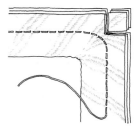

Inserting piping

Place the piping between the two layers of fabric with all four raw edges even. Pin, baste, and stitch in position using the zipper foot on the machine.

Turning corners

When attaching piping around a corner, cut a section out or clip into the seam allowance.

Fringe

1. Pin the solid part of the fringe to the turned-up edges.

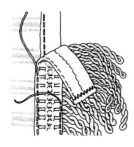

2. A light fringe can be held with two parallel lines of running stitch; a heavier fringe will require two rows of prickstitch.

Ruffles

1. Allow for the flat, ungathered ruffle to be one-and-a-half to two-and-a-half times the gathered width.

2. Cut the fabric strips twice the finished depth plus twice the seam allowance.

3. Mark out the ruffle strips on the straight grain. Cut and then join together with plain seams.

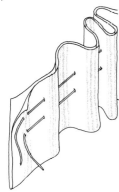

4. Fold in half length-wise and turn in ends.

5. Gather with two rows of stitches, with one just outside the seamline, and another halfway between raw edge and seamline.

6. Draw up to the required length.

7. To insert a ruffle between two layers, match raw edges and stitch along seamline.

Pleats

Pleats are often used for valances. Generous pleats will give a professional finish, but they must be carefully measured out. The width of the flat, ungathered fabric should be approximately three times the finished, pleated width for either box pleats or knife pleats.

1. It is important to trim away excess fabric, particularly when interlining is being used, to avoid bulky seams. Choose a fairly light interlining.

2. Cut out the fabric on the straight grain, being careful to match any pattern.

3. Calculate where box pleats will fall (see page 112) and allow for a size that will exactly cover the front of the valance shelf, ending neatly just short of the corners. The size can be altered by varying the space between the box pleats.

4. Divide the finished pleat length of the cornice by the pleat width to work out how many pleats will be needed.

5. Multiply the number of pleats by the amount of fabric needed for each pleat to find the ungathered width of the fabric.

6. Mark out with pins the pleat sections on the back of the valance, using a carpenter's square to mark parallel lines.

7. Any seamlines should be made to fall behind a pleat on a foldline.

For knife pleats, mark the foldlines. Make parallel pleats all folding to same side.

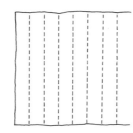

For box pleats, measure out the fabric as for knife pleats. The pleats point in alternating directions to form box pleats. Do not press them too flat; the folds should retain some elasticity.

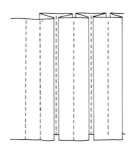

Mitering braids and ribbons

1. Baste the trimming along the first side, then stitch it along the top of the inner edge only up to the first corner.

2. At the first corner, fold the trimming back onto itself, right sides together.

3. Sew a diagonal line of stitching at precisely 45° between inner and outer corners. Trim

seam allowance and press open.

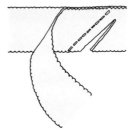

4. Repeat at each corner, then complete by stitching around the top of the outer edge.

Binding edges

1. The depth of a binding strip should be twice the finished depth plus twice the seam allowance.

2. Cut the binding strip on the fabric bias. Fold the strip and turn under the edges. Press.

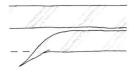

3. To bind a fabric edge, encase it inside the folded strip.

4. Hand sew in position or machine stitch close to the edge of the fold.

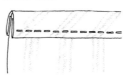

5. Alternatively, unfold one edge of the bias strip and place it along the fabric edge, with the raw edges even and the right sides together.

6. Stitch along the seamline, ⅝in (15mm) in from the edge.

7. Turn and press, pushing both seam allowances to the same side. Trim and

fold the bias strip over the raw edges.

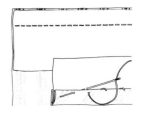

8. Turn under the edge in line with the previous stitching. Pin and slip stitch in position.

9. An equal band of binding should show on either side of the main fabric.

Mitering binding

1. Stitch the first side up to the corner point.

2. Fold the binding back over the stitched side so that the fold is in line with the edge.

3. Stitch the next side from the corner point.

4. When the binding has been stitched all around, turn it over the raw fabric edge, pressing the corners into the miters on both sides.

Calculating Yardages

These charts provide a quick yardage estimate for a pair of curtains made up in plain fabric. They allow for (2½ × fullness) a 3in (8cm) return, ⅝in (15mm) seams, plus 12in (30cm) for headings and hems. Extra fabric must be allowed for pattern repeats.

- ❑ Establish the number of widths required by using Chart One.
- ❑ Now establish the total yardage by using Chart Two.
- ❑ Here is a worked example for estimating yardages for curtains with the following measurements:
- ❑ Fabric width 54in
- ❑ Length of rod 58½in
- ❑ Finished length of curtains 85in
- ❑ For a fabric width of 54in and a track length of 58½in, the number of widths of fabric required falls between 3 and 4 widths on Chart One. However, 58½in is only 4½in larger than 54in (3 widths) whereas it is 16½in smaller than 75in (4 widths); therefore the number of widths required for a 58½in-long rod is 3.
- ❑ Moving on to Chart Two, the finished length of 85in is rounded up to 88in (the finished length must not be rounded down because this will result in insufficient fabric). Reading down the 3-width column, the yardage required is 8⅓yd.
- ❑ For all curtains, gathered valances, and balloon shades, the flat, ungathered width measurement (the distance along the hem) should be two-and-a-half times the finished width measurement (the distance along the heading).
- ❑ For a less voluminous effect, the ratio can be reduced.
- ❑ Curtain projects that use plain or small-patterned fabrics usually require the same amount of lining and interlining as face fabric. Large repeats often require less.

CHART ONE: CALCULATION OF NUMBER OF WIDTHS

Number of widths		**2**	**3**	**4**	**5**	**6**	**7**	**8**	**9**	**10**
Fabric 48in wide	Length of rod or pole (in)	29	46	65	81½	100	117	136	152½	171
Fabric 54in wide	Length of rod or pole (in)	34½	54	75	95	116	136	157	176	198
Fabric 60in wide	Length of rod or pole (in)	38½	60	83½	105	128	150	173	194½	218

CHART TWO: CALCULATION OF TOTAL YARDAGE

Number of widths		**2**	**3**	**4**	**5**	**6**	**7**	**8**	**9**	**10**
Finished length	40in	3	4⅓	5⅞	7¼	8⅔	10⅛	11⅝	13	14½
	44in	3⅛	4⅔	6¼	7⅞	9⅓	11	12½	14	15⅝
	48in	3⅓	5	6⅔	8⅓	10	11⅔	13⅓	15	16⅔
	52in	3⅝	5⅓	7⅛	9	10⅔	12½	14¼	16	17⅞
	56in	3⅞	5⅔	7⅝	9½	11⅓	13¼	15⅛	17	19
	60in	4	6	8	10	12	14	16	18	20
	64in	4¼	6⅓	8½	10⅝	12⅔	14⅞	17	19	21⅛
	68in	4½	6⅔	9	11⅛	13⅓	15⅝	17⅞	20	22¼
	72in	4⅔	7	9⅓	11⅔	14	16⅓	18⅔	21	23⅓
	76in	5	7⅓	9⅞	12¼	14⅔	17⅛	19⅝	22	24½
	80in	5⅛	7⅔	10¼	12⅞	15⅓	18	20½	23	25⅝
	84in	5¼	8	10⅔	13⅓	16	18⅔	21⅓	24	26⅔
	88in	5⅝	8⅓	11⅛	14	16⅔	19½	22¼	25	27⅞
	92in	5⅞	8⅔	11⅝	14½	17⅓	20¼	23⅛	26	29
	96in	6	9	12	15	18	21	24	27	30
	100in	6¼	9⅓	11⅝	15⅝	18⅔	21⅞	25	28	31⅛
	104in	6½	9⅔	13	16⅛	19⅓	22⅝	25⅞	29	32¼
	108in	6⅔	10	13⅓	16⅔	20	23⅓	26⅔	30	33⅓
	112in	7	10⅓	13⅞	17¼	20⅔	24⅛	27⅝	31	34¼
	116in	7⅛	10⅔	14¼	17⅞	21⅓	25	28½	32	35⅝
	120in	7⅓	11	14⅔	18⅓	22	25⅔	29⅓	33	36⅔
	124in	7⅝	11⅓	15⅛	19	22⅔	26½	30¼	34	37⅞
	128in	7⅞	11⅔	15⅝	19½	23⅓	27¼	31⅛	35	39
	132in	8	12	16	20	24	28	32	36	40
	136in	8¼	12⅓	16½	20⅝	24⅔	28⅞	33	37	41⅛
	140in	8½	12⅔	17	21⅛	25⅓	29⅝	33⅞	38	42¼

Care and Maintenance

Curtainmaking can be a time-consuming and expensive business. A little care will preserve your investment. Foresight is also vital. For example, avoid pale and delicate fabrics in a room where children or dogs roam free. A sensible choice of fabric and treatment will allow your curtains, drapes, and shades a long life and spare you anxiety.

DRY CLEANING
❑ Few curtains or shades can be hand- or machine-washed.
❑ Linings and face fabrics, as well as tapes and other trimmings, may shrink, or lose body, color, and finish. Check the selvage of your fabric for cleaning instructions. Always use the best dry cleaner available. Many offer a comprehensive service that involves removing, cleaning, mending if necessary, rehanging, and training.
❑ Fabric protectors are available to treat material before or after making up, rendering the surface less prone to absorbing liquids. Some fabrics are already treated in this way – check the selvage for information.
❑ Before purchasing a costly fabric (e.g. green baize), first buy a small length and ask a cleaner to test it.
❑ Always use pre-shrunk piping cord.

WASHING
❑ Most fabrics, including linings, are liable to shrink. Before making up any project:
1. Leave a large hem for turning down later.
2. Check that the fabric is pre-shrunk, testing a small piece if necessary.
3. If not, wash the fabric before making

up. Iron while damp.
❑ Some dry cleaners will pre-shrink the material for you by passing it over steam. This is the best method. Washing can cause loss of body and will remove any finish, e.g. a glaze.
❑ Muslins and sheers will yellow or turn gray with age; only washing will restore brilliance. Muslin, however, will lose body and shrink.

Stains
❑ It is vital to act fast in case of a stain. Scrape off any excess – do not rub it in. Blot up wet marks and dust any powdery stains. Test a corner before treating a stain. Use water at room temperature – as hot water may set a stain. Water should not be used on silk or wool – it can easily cause both shrinkage and color loss.
❑ Take care to use the correct solvent for the fabric and the stain.

PROBLEMS
Fabric glue
❑ Fabric glue can be remobilized in the dry cleaning process. Be sure to check the instructions on the bottle. If necessary, replace the glue after cleaning. Sew any trimmings into place rather than using glue.

Finishes
❑ Glazes on chintzes are easily damaged. Try to avoid wrinkling and handling.
❑ A watered effect, such as moiré, disappears easily if splashed with water. Some man-made moirés, however, are unaffected by water.
❑ Use a traverse rod or special ring-pulls with a pole to keep handling of the leading edges to a minimum.

Fusible buckrams
❑ Fusible buckrams are impregnated with glue that is released with ironing. The dry cleaning process causes the glue to be remobilized so headings, tiebacks, or cornices, stiffened with a fusible buckram, tend to crinkle and lose body. Washing such materials will have a still more disastrous effect. Sew-in, non-fusible buckrams can be cleaned, however.

Interlinings
❑ Cotton interlinings can be dry cleaned without problem; synthetic interlinings sometimes lose their shape. Neither should ever be washed.

Linings
❑ Cotton linings can be dry cleaned and, if detachable, washed.

Care of Fabrics
Washing symbols and care labels
Always use the recommended care label advice to achieve the best results.
Red = Do not do/use
Yellow = Use caution
Green = Go ahead

 Do not wash. RED

 Hand wash gently in lukewarm water. YELLOW

 Machine wash in cold water using mild detergent. YELLOW

 Machine wash in lukewarm water (up to 100°F, 40°C) at a delicate setting using mild detergent. YELLOW

 Machine wash in warm water at a delicate setting. YELLOW

 Machine wash in warm water (up to 120°F, 50°C) at a normal setting. GREEN

 Machine wash in hot water (not exceeding 160°F, 70°C) at a normal setting. GREEN

 Dry on flat surface after removing excess water. GREEN

 Do not tumble dry. RED

 Tumble dry at a low temperature and remove article from machine as soon as it is dry. YELLOW

 "Drip" dry – hang soaking wet. GREEN

 Tumble dry at a medium to high temperature and remove from machine as soon as it is dry. GREEN

 Hang to dry after removing excess water. GREEN

 Do not use chlorine bleach. RED

 Use chlorine bleach with care. Follow package directions. RED

 Do not iron. RED

 Iron at a high temperature (up to 390°F, 200°C). GREEN

 Do not dry clean. RED

 Professionally dry clean. GREEN

❑ Blackout and aluminum-coated linings can be dry cleaned but not washed.

Roller shades
❑ Do not wash or dry these shades.

Roman shades
❑ Attempt washing only if the shade is made from pre-washed, pre-shrunk fabric. Always be very careful to remove any brass rings or lead weights.

Glossary

NOTE: For fabrics, linings, and stiffeners see Fabric Glossary on page 80. For hand stitches see Sewing Techniques on page 178.

Awl
A pointed tool that makes holes in wood surfaces.

Balloon shade
A shade that has fullness in the width, sometimes formed into inverted pleats, and is raised and lowered by cords threaded through rings at the back.

Bay window
A window consisting of three adjacent windows projecting from the building and forming an alcove inside.

Bow window
A rounded *bay window*.

Brackets
Supports for either a *rod, pole, shade,* or *valance shelf*.

Buckram
An interfacing used as a *stiffener* inside handmade curtain, drapery, and valance *headings*, as well as *tiebacks* and *cornices*. Made from cotton or jute, it is available in different weights, in fusible and sew-in versions; it is normally 4in (10cm) wide.

Cascade
Pleated fabric that hangs at either side of a *swag*.

Casement window
A window with one or more sashes that are hinged on a vertical edge.

Cornice
A decorative structure with a flat surface, mounted above a window to hide the curtain rod and the top of the curtain or drapery. Made from painted plywood or from plywood or *buckram* covered with fabric, it can have either a straight or a shaped edge. Unlike a *valance*, it is firm.

Covered cornice board
A narrow strip of *buckram* or plywood covered with fabric and tacked to the front edge of a *valance shelf* to hide a curtain rod or shade mounting board.

Craft knife
Tool with a sharp, V-shaped, replaceable blade, useful for cutting heavy *buckram* or any other very stiff materials.

Curtain
A window covering to floor- or sill-length, usually with fullness in the width, which is sometimes hung alone or on one side of a window but more often is used in pairs. It hangs from a *rod* or *pole* by means of hooks or tabs or is slotted onto a rod. A term often used to mean a *drapery*.

Decorator tape
Tape that is stitched to the top of a curtain to create a *gathered heading* or *pinch pleats* either by pulling cords running through the tape or by inserting special *pleater hooks*.

Dormer window
A window, usually small, set into the slope of a roof and projecting from it.

Double-hung window
A window consisting of an upper sash and a lower sash that slide vertically. The sashes may be divided into panes.

Drapery
A heavy, full-length curtain with a pleated *heading*; the term is often shortened to "drape." It is also used to mean draped fabric such as a *swag*.

Dress curtains
Curtains that are never intended to be drawn; used for decorative purposes only.

Face fabric
The principal fabric of curtains or draperies, facing the interior of the room.

Finials
The decorative end pieces of a *pole*.

Finished length
The length from top edge to base edge of a finished curtain, drapery, shade, valance, or cornice.

Finished width
The width of the finished *heading*, after pleating or gathering.

Flat curtain rod
A curtain rod not operated by a cord and pulley as a *traverse rod* is.

French doors
A pair of doors with glass panes for most or all of their length.

Gathered heading
A curtain or valance heading gathered using *gathering tape*.

Gathering tape
A *decorator tape* in which cords are pulled up to create a gathered effect (using narrow, two-cord gathering tape) or *pencil pleats* (using a wider gathering tape).

Glass curtains
Sheer *undercurtains* hanging behind the main curtains.

Goblet pleats
Pinch pleats with the top edge pushed out and padded to form a goblet shape.

Heading
The top of a *curtain, drapery, valance,* or *balloon shade* which hangs from a *rod* or *pole*. Headings range from simple, unpleated tabs to handmade pleats backed by hooks. They are often made using *decorator tape* to form *pinch pleats* or *gathered headings*.

Holdback
An ornamental wood or metal shape attached to the wall on either side of a window near a curtain or drapery, which is looped over the holdback when open.

Hook-and-loop tape
Self-gripping tape that comes in sew-on and self-adhesive forms. It is mainly used to attach a *cornice* or *valance* to the front edge of the *valance shelf*; the "hook" side is stuck to the shelf, the "loop" side is sewn to the valance or cornice.

Hourglass curtain

A *sash curtain* tied at the center to create a "waisted" effect.

Interlining

A soft layer of cloth placed between the *face fabric* and *lining* to provide insulation and also improve the way the curtain or drapery hangs.

Interlocking

A method of linking layers of *face fabric*, *interlining*, and *lining* using long, loose stitches known as lockstitch.

Lambrequin

A flat, stiff *cornice* extending down each side of the window; the inner edge frames the window.

Leading edges

Inner vertical edges of a pair of curtains or draperies.

Lining

Backing fabric of a curtain, drapery, or shade.

Miter

A corner fold, usually in the hem.

Padded edge

Leading edge of a curtain or drapery containing a roll of padding to create a distinctive and luxurious effect.

Pencil pleats

Narrow, regular pleats in the *heading* of a curtain or balloon shade. They can be made by hand, but are generally formed using *decorator tape*.

Pinch pleats

Regularly spaced triple pleats, used for curtain, drapery, or valance *headings*. They can be formed by hand or using a *decorator tape* that either pulls up with cords or has pockets for special *pleater hooks*.

Pleater hooks

Pronged hooks used with *pleater tape* to make *pinch pleats*. When the prongs are slotted into the pockets in the tape and pinched together, they form a pleat.

Pleater tape

A *decorator tape* used with *pleater hooks* to create *pinch pleats*.

Pole

A brass, wrought iron, or wood rod that has a decorative *finial* at each end and is supported by *brackets*. Curtains are hung from the pole.

Poufed heading

The stand-up part of the fabric above a *gathered heading* or a *rod-pocket heading*, which is teased out to form a fat ruffle.

Reefing

A pair of *stationary curtains* in which the *leading edges* are pulled back like theater curtains, by means of diagonally strung cords.

Repeat

The vertical distance between each repeated motif of the pattern of a fabric.

Return

The part of a *curtain*, *drapery*, *cornice*, or *valance* that goes around the side. To hang flush with the wall at right angles, it is usually equivalent to the distance between the front surface and the wall.

Rod

A rail or track from which a *curtain*, *drapery*, or sometimes a *valance* is hung. A *traverse rod* is operated with a cord and pulley system, and curtains on a *flat curtain rod* are opened and closed by hand.

Rod-pocket curtain

A curtain where the top forms a pocket which is gathered onto a rod or pole.

Roller shade

A shade of stiffened fabric, usually operated by a spring mechanism, that rolls up above the window.

Roman shade

A flat shade with dowels slotted horizontally up the back, so it can easily be pulled up into soft horizontal folds.

Sash curtain

Rod-pocket curtain with a second pocket gathered onto a rod, at the base of the curtain. They are usually *sheer*.

Shade

A fabric window covering that can be pulled up on a roller or pleated up vertically. See *balloon*, *roller*, and *Roman shades*.

Sheers

Curtains made from sheer fabric.

Skylight

A window in a roof or ceiling.

Slat

A long, flat piece of wood used at the base of either a *roller* or *Roman shade*.

Smocked heading

A handmade heading imitating smocking, in which the pleats are alternately linked to form a honeycomb pattern.

Smocking tape

A *decorator tape* in which two cords are pulled to create an effect very similar to gathering.

Stackback

The space taken up by pleated curtains or draperies when open; it is also the area on either side of a window, where curtains or draperies are stacked back.

Stationary curtains/ draperies

Curtains/draperies in which the *heading* does not move; they may be held open by *tiebacks*, *holdbacks*, or *reefing*, or they may be sheer curtains that are permanently closed, such as a *sash curtain*.

Stiffener

Interfacing such as crinoline or *buckram* used to stiffen handmade curtain, shade, or valance *headings*, *tiebacks*, or *cornices*.

Swag

A sweeping drape at the top of a window, appearing to hang from points at either side. The term is often used to include the *cascades* that hang at the sides.

Tape

A strip of fabric used in the construction of curtains. *Decorator tape* is used in making some *headings*, while *hook-and-loop tape* is used to attach a *cornice* or *valance* to a *valance shelf.* Twill tape, or web, is sometimes used to reinforce a handmade heading.

Tieback

A band, cord, ribbon, chain, or other means of tying back a curtain to the wall.

Traverse rod

A rod that allows the curtains or draperies to be operated by a cord and pulley. A two-way traverse rod operates two curtains/draperies in opposite directions at once.

Undercurtains

Curtains that hang behind the main curtains or draperies.

Valance

A gathered or pleated panel that hangs above the curtain to hide the curtain *rod.* An attached valance is attached to the top of the curtain, but other types usually hang from the front edge of a *valance shelf.* Unlike a *cornice,* a valance is not rigid.

Valance shelf

A board mounted above a window at right angles to the wall like a shelf. One or more *rods,* a *cornice,* a *valance,* a *swag,* or a *covered cornice board* may be attached to it.

Weights

Round pieces of lead-like metal, pierced with two holes in the center and used to weight hems of curtains, draperies, and shades so that they hang better. Covered chain weights are a form of weighted tape used in the hems of *sheer* curtains.

Welting

Piping cord covered in fabric and sewn around the edges, often into the seams, of tiebacks, valances, curtains, etc, for decoration.

Bibliography

Authentic Decor
Peter Thornton
Outlet Book
Company, 1993

The Batsford Book of Soft Furnishings
Angela Fishburn
Trafalgar Square, 1985

The Book of Soft Furnishings
Charmian Watkins
Parkwest Publications, 1991

The Cabinet-Maker and Upholsterer's Guide
George Hepplewhite
Dover Publications, 1969

The Complete Book of Curtains and Drapes
Lady Caroline Wrey
Overlook Press, 1991

The Complete Book of Soft Furnishings
Dorothy Gates, Eileen Kittier, and Susan Locke
Sterling Publishing, 1993

Curtains and Draperies
Jenny Gibbs
Overlook Press, 1994

Decorative Style Most Original
Kevin McCloud
Simon & Schuster, 1990

Early American Stencil Designs
Charlene Tarbox
Dover Publications, 1994

The Elements of Style
Ed. Stephen Calloway
Mitchell Beazley, 1991

Fabric Magic
Melanie Paine
Pantheon Books, 1992

Finishing Touches
Elizabeth Hilliard
Crown Publishing, 1991

Furnish with Fabric
Tricia Guild
Crown Publishing, 1991

House into Home
Mary Gilliatt
Random House, 1992

Laura Ashley Complete Guide to Home Decorating
Crown Publishing, 1992

Laura Ashley Guide to Country Decorating
Lorrie Mack, Lucinda Egerton, and Jane Newdick
Hyperion, 1993

The New House Book
Terence Conran
Outlet Book
Company, 1989

Painted Furniture Patterns
Jocasta Innes and Stewart Walton
Studio Books, 1994

Soft Furnishing for the Bedroom
Angela Fishburn
Trafalgar Square, 1990

Soft Furnishings
Pat Ross
Meredith Books, 1992

Terence Conran's Home Furnishings
Terence Conran
Outlet Book
Company, 1989

Tricia Guild on Colour
Tricia Guild
Rizzoli, 1993

Upholstery
Dorothy Gates
Sterling Publishing, 1990

Index

Page numbers in *italics*
refer to picture
captions.

accessories 166, *166–7*
acetate 80
aluminum-coated
  thermal linings 83
arched windows *16*,
  16–17, 120, *120, 126*

backstitch 179
baize curtains 81
balloon shades and
  curtains 13, *40*, 142,
  150
  for arched windows 16,
    16
  for bay windows 13
  in child's room 152,
    152
  fringed *79*
  making and fitting
    150–1, 176
  measuring for 87, 88
  muslin *16*, 153, *153*
  silk 152
basting 180
bathrooms 45, *45*
batik curtains 81
batting 83
bay windows *12, 58*
  curtains for 12, *12*
  mounting rods in 12,
    175
  poles for 168, 171
  shades for 13
bedrooms 38, *38–41, 50,
  55, 67*
  children's *12*, 43, *13*
bias strips, cutting 182
binding edges 183
blackout linings 83
blind-catchstitch 179
blinds
  rattan *45*
  Venetian *27, 38*
block-printing 156–7,
  157
borders 76, *76, 137*
  see also edges
bouclé *72*
bows 126, 158, *158*
  false 159
  Swedish (headings)
    103, *103*
bow windows 13, *13*
  false poles for 168, 171

mounting rods in 13,
  175
box pleats 183
brackets, fitting:
  for cornices 175
  for poles 171, 173
braids 76, *76*
  broad 77
  linen and seersucker
    78
  mitering 183
  viscose and cotton *77,
    78*
brocade curtains *46*, 68,
  81, 82
buckram
  fusible 83, 90, 91, 96
  heavyweight 83
  non-fusible 83, 91, 96
button tufts *78*

cable top headings 102,
  102
canvas *48*
cascades 128–9, 131; *see
  also* swags
ceilings, attaching to
  169
chain weights, covered
  91, *166*
checked curtains *18, 32,
  40*, 48, *48, 50, 58, 63*,
  81, 100, 134
checked shades *40*, 142,
  145
cheesecloth 81
children's rooms 42, 43,
  43
  shade for 152, *152*
chintz curtains 10, 76,
  81, *85*
  large-scale prints 56,
    58
  modern prints *60*
  plain *48*
  small-scale prints 52,
    54
choux 126, *126*, 132,
  133, 158, 160, *160*
cleaning and
  maintenance 11, 80,
  90, 92, 185
collage 136
color 11
concrete, attaching to
  169
contrasting edges 161
  bias strips for 182
cord, shade *166*
corded rods 174, 175

see also reefing
cording, decorative 94,
  96, 97, 100, *100*, 134
cornice boards, covered
  87, 118, 169, 175
cornices 108, 120, *124*
  buckram for 83
  draped *40*
  embroidered 163, *163*
  fringed 76
  gilded *15*
  Gothic *120–1*, 120–2
  Grecian urn 123, *123*
  lining for 94
  measuring for 87
  pagoda 124, *124*
  painted, with tassels
    125, *125*
  picture rails and 87
  for picture windows 20
  plaid 122, *122*
  scalloped *78*
  serpentine *58*
  stenciled *28*
  striped 123, *123*
  wood *34, 92*
  zigzag *148*, 148–9
  see also valance shelves;
    valances
cotton 39, 72, 80
  checked and striped
    18, 45, 48, *48, 62, 63*
  curtains *18, 45, 50*, 103
  floral 56
  large-scale prints 56,
    56, 58–9
  Madras 82
  modern prints 60, *60,
    62–3*
  plain 48, *48*
  Provençal 52, *52*
  shades *40*
  small-scale prints 52,
    52, 54–5
  translucent 64, *64, 79,
    90*
  valances *39*
cotton duck 81, 136
cotton lawn 81
cotton sateen 83
cotton velvet 82
couching 163, *163*
crewelwork 81
crinoline 96
curtain and drapery
  projects:
  interlined 94–5
  lined 92–3
  no-sew 136, *137*
  unlined 90–1

see also balloon shades
  and curtains;
  headings, curtain;
  interlinings; linings;
  pull-up curtains;
  reefing; swags and
  cascades; tiebacks
cutting fabric 89, 178

damask 68, 81
  curtains *58*, 68, *72*
  shade *71*
dining rooms 33, *33–7,
  66, 67*
door curtains 20, *25, 33,
  72*
doors:
  French 10, *18*, 19, *36*
  sliding glass 20
dormer windows 14,
  14–15
  poles for 14, *20*, 173
dotted Swiss *64*, 82
double-hung windows
  19, *19*
drafts, preventing 11,
  20, 24, 25
draperies *see* curtain
  and drapery projects
drawn work *17*
duck, cotton 81, 136
dupion 81

edges and edgings:
  binding 183
  contrasting 161, 182
  fan *77, 78*
  finishing raw 181
  padded 128, 158, 161
  scalloped cotton *78*
  see also braids; fringes;
    welting and piping
electrical wiring 169
embroidered curtains:
  Baroque 163, *163*
  drawn work *17*
  Kashmiri *60*
  translucent 64, *64*
embroidered swagged
  valance *27*
eyelet 81

fabrics:
  buying 11, 89
  calculating yardage
    for, 88
  cutting 89, 178
  glossary of 80–3
  measuring 86–7
  see also patterned

fabrics
fading of fabrics 11
fan edgings *77, 78*
fan-pleated headings
  107
fan shade 153
fashion and style 10
felt, table or reinforced
  83
fibers 80
finials 168, 170, *170,
  171, 172*
flannel interlining 83
flat-fell seams 181
fleece, needle-punched
  83
floral designs 52, *54*, 56,
  58, 59
flutes *131*
French doors 10, *18*, 19,
  36
French pleats 97, *97*
French seams 181
fringes *58, 70*, 76, *76*
  attaching 182–3
  beaded 76
  bullion 76, *77, 78*
  cotton *78*
  linen 128
  pompom *40, 78, 79,
    90, 126*
  tassel *77*
  on valances *34*

gathered headings 28,
  38, 99, *99*, 107
gathering stitch 180
gimp 77
gingham 48, *48*, 81
  curtains *50*
  shades *40*, 142, 145
glass curtain *66 see also*
  sheers
goblet pleats 97, *97*
Gothic cornices *120–1*,
  120–2
Grecian urn cornices
  123, *123*
grain, fabric 178
grosgrain 81
  bows 158

hall curtains 24, 25, *25*
hanging curtains 91, 93,
  95, 177
headings, curtain:
  cable top 102, *102*
  cased 99, *99*
  corded 100, *100*
  fan-pleated 107

flopped forward 30
French-pleated 97, *97*
fusible 83
gathered *28*, *38*, 99,
   99, 107
goblet-pleated 97, *97*
handmade 90, 91, 93,
   95, 96
   machine-stitched 91,
     93, 95, 96, 107
pencil-pleated *96*, 98,
   98, 103, 107
pinch-pleated *39*, *96*,
   97, *97*, 107
poufed 99, 104
rod-pocket *75*, 99, *103*,
   104, 104–5, *105*, 173
scalloped 99
with self-ruffle 91, 99,
   104, 105
smocked *98*, *98*, 107
Swedish bow 103, *103*
tab *42*, *50*, 99, 102, *102*
tapes for 90, 91, 93, 95,
   107
tied 99, 100–1, *101*
unpleated 99, *99*, 136
zigzag 103, *103*
heat loss, preventing 20,
   24, *25*
hems:
   fringed *70*
   mitering corners
     181–2
   weighting 91
herringbone weave *48*
holdbacks *55*, 105, 166
holland 81
hook-and-loop tape 107,
   166
hooks, curtain 95, 98,
   107, *166*
hourglass curtains *33*,
   66

ikat 81
Indian embroidered
   cotton *60*
Indian handwoven slub
   48
Indian saris *67*
interlined curtains *18*,
   89, 92, 94–5
interlining materials 83
ironing curtains 89, 177

jacquard *72*

kilims *36*
kitchen curtains and

shades 11, *32*, 33, *33*,
   55, 86, 100, 142
knife pleats 183

lace 82
   curtains *10*, *33*, 64, *64*,
     66, 82
   valances *14*, 15
ladderstitch 89, 179–80
lambrequins 15, 21, *25*,
   72, 108, 125, *125*
lawn, cotton 81
lawn, muslin 82
length, curtain 86
   for interlined curtains
     94
   for lined curtains 93
   for unlined curtains 91
light, exclusion of 11
lined curtains *92*, 92–3
   washing 92
linen 48, *48*, 80
   and cotton mixtures
     (union) *72*, 82
   curtains *76*, 80
   fringe *76*, *78*, *79*
   large-scale prints 56,
     56, 58–9
   small-scale prints *52*
lining bags 91
linings 89, 92
   aluminum-coated
     thermal 83
   blackout 83
   cotton sateen 83
   detachable 92, 107
   locking in 93, 95
   making curtains with
     92–3, 94–5
   patterned *92*
   for swags and cascades
     126
living rooms 11, 26,
   26–9, *58*, *67*, 108
locking in: interlinings
   94, 95
   linings 93, 95
lockstitch 94, 95, 180

Madras cotton 82
Maltese crosses 126,
   158, 159, *159*
marquisette 82
measuring 86–9
   for cornices 87
   for curtains 86–7
   and pattern-matching
     89
   for pinch pleats 97
   for rod position 87

for shades 87–8
for swags and cascades
   88
for tiebacks 87
for valances 87
mitering:
   braids and ribbons 183
   hems 181–2
moiré silk *68*, 82
muslin 64, *64*, 81
   curtains *16*, *20*, *38*, 43,
     45, *66*, *67*, 103, 107,
     132, *133*
   shades 153
   valances *43*, *67*
muslin lawn 82

no-sew curtains 136, *137*

organza, silk 64, *64*
overcasting 180

padded edges 128, 158,
   161
pagoda cornices 124,
   124
painting:
   of cornices 125, *125*
   of fabric *156*
   see also block-printing;
     stenciling
paisley fabrics *47*, *74*,
   75, 82
patterned fabrics:
   cutting 178
   large-scale prints 56,
     56, 58–9, *72*
   matching pattern 89
   modern 60, *60*, 62–3
   small-scale prints 52,
     52, 54–5
   see also block-printing;
     paisley; plaid fabrics;
     stenciling
pencil pleats *96*, 98, *98*,
   103
   tape for 107
percale, Provençal *52*
periods, mixing 10
pinch pleats *96*, 97, *97*
   tape for 107
   in valances *39*
pinking shears *166*
pipes *131*
piping *78*, 182
plaid fabrics
   cornice 122, *122*
   curtains *72*, 72, 80, 82
plaster walls, attaching
   to 169

pleats
   French, handmade 97,
     97
   machine-stitched 107
   pencil, handmade *96*,
     98, *98*, 103
   pinch, handmade *39*,
     96, 97, *97*
   for valances *39*, 183
plush *72*, *74*, 82
poles 87, 168, 170
   brackets and sockets
     for *166*, 171, 173
   brass *50*, *52*, 103, 171,
     171, 172, *172*
   chrome 171, 172, *172*
   doorway *20*, 173
   dormer *14*, *20*, 173
   draped *29*, *38*, 126
   false 171
   finials for 168, 170,
     170, 171, *172*
   fitting 168, 169, 171,
     173
   gilded *70*
   lubricating 172
   rings for *166*, 168, 171
   for skylights *14*
   steel *36*
   wood *28*, 171, *172*,
     172–3
   wrought-iron *35*, 172,
     172
pompom fringes *40*, *78*,
   79, 90, 126
poufed headings 99,
   104
prickstitch 180
prints:
   large-scale 56, *56*,
     58–9, *72*
   modern 60, *60*, 62–3
   small-scale 52, *52*, 54–5
projects see curtain and
   drapery projects
Provençal cottons 52, *52*
pull-up curtains *40*, 150

radiators *21*, *40*
rattan blinds *45*
rayon see viscose
reefing 16, *34*, 134–5,
   176
Regency style *9*, *27*, *38*
repeats 89
ribbons, mitering 183
rings, curtain *166*, 168,
   171
rod-pocket curtains *75*,
   99, *103*, *104*, 104–5,

105, 134
attaching to pole 173
rods:
   bendable 12, 13, 16
   curtain/drapery 174
   decorative traverse 171
   flat 174, *174*, 175
   mounting 169, 175
   multiple 175
   position 87
   for sheers 174, *174*,
     175
   traverse 174, *174*, 175
   see also reefing
roller shades *40*, 142,
   143
   for French doors *19*
   making and fitting
     143, *143*, 176
   measuring for 87–8
   undertensioned 176
roll-up shades 145
Roman shades *32*, *42*,
   45, *59*, *63*, 142, 146
   making and fitting
     146–8, 176
   measuring for 87, 88
   stained glass 149, *149*
   stenciling *154*, 154–5
   uses for 13, 20, 21
   zigzag with matching
     cornice *148*, 148–9
rosettes *78*, 87, 126, 158,
   160
ruffled headings:
   positioning tape for 91
   poufed 99, 104, 105
ruffles, making 183

saris, Indian *67*
sash curtains 16
sateen 82
   curtains *60*
   linings 83
scalloped cornices *78*
scalloped headings 99
screw eyes *166*
seams:
   allowance 178
   clipping 181
   at corners 181
   flat-fell 181
   French 181
   plain 181
selvages, trimming 93,
   94, 181
sewing 89, 178
   see stitches, hand
shade backing,
   fusible 143

shades 142 (see balloon shades and curtains; roller shades; roll-up shades; Roman shades
for arched windows 16, *16*, 17
for bathrooms 45, *45*
for bay windows 13
in bedrooms 38, 40, 42, *43*
for children's rooms 42, 152, *152*
with curtains *20*, 40, *54*, *59*, 110, 116, 117, 131, 176
damask *71*
for dormer windows 15
for French doors 19
in kitchens *32*, *33*
for picture windows 20
pleated *17*
for skylights 14
for small windows 15
for tall, narrow windows *17*
shantung silk 82
shawls, antique, as valances 38
sheers 64, *64*, 82
sash rods for 174, *174*, 175
tape for 107
shutters 21, 35
silk 68, 80, 82
curtains 11, *36*, *40*, *47*, *64*, *68*, *70*, *71*, *72*, *96*, 105, 126
shades 152, *152*
swags *126*, 128–9
see also dupion
sill-length curtains 86, 87, *92*
skylights 14, *14*
sliding glass doors 20
slip stitch 180
slub, Indian hand-woven *48*
smocked headings 98, *98*
spirals *131*
spray, stiffening 143
stackback 87
staircase curtains 25, *25*, *54*
staple gun *166*
stationary curtains and draperies 11, 17, *55*, 87, 97, 98, 134
stenciling:
of cornices 28

of curtains 102
of shades *154*, 154–5
stiffening spray 143
stitches, hand:
backstitch 179
basting 180
blind-catchstitch 179
gathering 180
ladderstitch 179–80
lockstitch 178, 180
overcasting 180
prickstitch 180
slip stitch 180
striped curtains and shades *35*, *36*, *38*, *42*, *45*, 48, *48*, *54*, *55*, *58*, *62*, *70*, 131
striped cornices 123, *123*
stripes, painting 156, *156*
studies 30, *30–1*
style 10
swagged valances 27, 130, *130*
swags *9*, 10, *12*, *19*, *25*, *70*, 76, 126
Art Deco 131, *131*
cutting patterns for 128
fitting 177
measuring for 88
muslin curtains with 132, *133*
silk *126*, 128–9
on valances 130, *130*
Swedish bows 103, *103*
swing arms 14, *20*
Swiss, dotted *64*, 82

tab curtains *16*, *42*, *50*, 102, *102*
taffeta 82
curtains *70*
tapes:
chain weight 91, *166*
heading 90, 91, 93, 95, 107
hook-and-loop 107, *166*
lining 92, 107
tapestry fabric 72, 82
tassel valance 162, *162*
tassels *28*, *47*, *70*, *75*, 76, 77, *96*
ticking 48, 82
tiebacks *23*, 128, 138, *140*
attaching to hooks 139
buckram for 83

crescent *138*, 139
cutting 87
edged with fringes and braids *78*
hooks for 169
measuring for 87
pencil-pleated 140, *140*
pocket 141, *141*
position of 138
roses 141, *141*
ruched 139, *139*
ruffled 140, *140*
tassel *70*, 76, 77, 108
tied curtains 100–1, *101*
toile de Jouy *56*, 82
tools and accessories 166, *166–7*
training curtains 91, 93, 95, *177*
translucent curtains 11, *29*, 64, *64*, 66–7, 90
traverse rods 174, *174*, 175
trimmings 76, *76–9*, 158–63
attaching 182–3
tussah silk 82, 128

undercurtains *58*, *75*, 104
union, linen 82
unlined curtains 90–1
unpleated curtains 99, *99*, 136

valance shelves 168
covering 169
mounting 169, 175
see also cornice boards, covered
valances 108
arched *116*, 116–17
attached 35, *118*, 118–19
bell-pleated damask 108–9, *109*
box-pleated 112–13, *113*, 183
gathered *50*, *52*, *92*, 114
improvised *33*, *38*, *67*
knife-pleated 183
lace *14*, 15
lining 94
measuring for 87
muslin *67*
pinch-pleated *39*
ruched bell-pleated *110*, 110–11

serpentine *34*, *76*, 108, *114*, 114–15
swagged 27, 130, *130*
tassel 162, *162*
see also cornices; lambrequins
velvet 68, *68*, 72, *72*, 82
brocade 82
cornice 72
curtains and draperies *63*, 72, *75*, 161
gaufraged 82
lambrequins 72
padded edges for 158, 161
Venetian blinds 27, 38
vine eyes *166*
viscose 80
embroidered *68*
trimmings 77
velvet 72
voile 64, *64*, 83
curtains *33*, *45*, 99

wall coverings, matching *59*
wall structure and surfaces 169
washing see cleaning and maintenance
weights, inserting 91
width, curtain 86
for interlined curtains 94
for lined curtains 93
for unlined curtains 91
widths, joining 91, 93, 94
windows:
arched *16*, 16–17, *126*
bay see bay windows
bow see bow windows
differently sized 20, *20*
dormer *14*, 14–15
double-hung 19, *19*
inaccessible 21
inward-opening *10*, *50*
lacking space around *20*, 21
picture 20, *20*, *28*, 39
skylight 14, *14*
small 15, *15*, *55*
staircase 25, *25*, *54*
tall and narrow 17, *17*
see also French doors and sliding glass doors
window seats 13, 21, 142
wood, screwing into 169
wool 72, 80

curtains *75*
see also plaid fabrics
workrooms 30, *30–1*

zigzag cornices, with Roman shades *148*, 148–9
zigzag headings 103, *103*

Acknowledgments

AUTHOR'S ACKNOWLEDGMENTS

I would like to express my deepest gratitude to the following people for their invaluable professional help or personal support: my editor, Denny Hemming – without whom this book would never have been written; Rosalie Beaumont; Elizabeth Forbes; Christophe and Fanny Forbes; Justine Ford; Brigid Juhanson; Di Morley; John Hardy; Anita Hildreth; Ruth White; Nadine Bazar; Nick Protts of L & S Services; Tony Helyer; May Povey; Alan Wharton and Paul Battle of F. R. Street Ltd; Graham Doyle of Pilgrim Payne; David Richardson of The Blinds Company; Francesca Scoones of The National Trust; Catherine Merrick and Rebecca Day, authors of *The Curtain Design Directory*; and Paul Semple, Librarian of the London School of Furniture. I reserve special thanks for my husband, William, who provided unfailing support.

I am also grateful to the numerous firms that have lent material for photography:

FABRICS: 52–3, 64–5, 72–3 Laura Ashley; 52–3, 56–7 Bennison; 64–5, 68–9 Celia Birtwell; 52–3 Nina Campbell; 48–9, 52–3, 56–7, 68–9 Manuel Canovas; 68–9 Rupert Cavendish; 48–9 Jane Churchill; 48–9, 52–3, 56–7 Colefax & Fowler; 56–7, 60–1 Collier Campbell; 48–9, 60–1, 64–5, 72–3 The Conran Shop; 48–9, 52–3, 60–1, 78 Designers Guild; 56–7 Christian Fischbacher; 52–3, 56–7, 64–5 Anna French; 68–9, 72–3 Guy Evans Ltd; 60–1 Pierre Frey; 48–9, 52–3, 60–1 Habitat; 48–9, 52–3, 56–7, 60–1, 64–5, 66–7, 68–9, 78, 166–7 John Lewis; 52–3, 60–1, 72–3 Liberty; 48–9 Ian Mankin; 76, 78 Henry Newbery & Co. Ltd; 48–9, 52–3, 56–7, 68–9, 76, 78 Osborne and Little; 64–5, 72–3 Percheron; 68–9 Sacho Hesslein; 52–3, 60–1 Souleiado; 64–5 John Stephanides; 83, 166–7 F.R. Street Ltd; 60–1, 72–3 Timney Fowler; 68–9, 72–3 Watts & Co.; 76 Wemyss Houles Ltd.

POLES & RODS: 172–3 Artisan; 172–3 The Bradley Collection; 137 Byron & Byron; 172–3 Hang-Ups Accessories Ltd; 172–3 McKinney Kidston; 174 Swish Products Ltd; 174 Cope and Timmings Ltd. TAPES: 166–7 Rufflette Ltd.

THE PUBLISHER WOULD LIKE TO THANK THE FOLLOWING PHOTOGRAPHERS AND ORGANIZATIONS FOR THEIR KIND PERMISSION TO REPRODUCE PHOTOGRAPHS IN THIS BOOK: 1 Ingalill Snitt; 3 IPC Magazines Ltd/Robert Harding Syndication; 4 center Marie Claire Maison/Dugied/Postic, 5 above Courtesy of Designers Guild, photograph by David Montgomery; 5 below Deidi von Schaewen; 6 below left Paul Ryan/International Interiors; 6 below right IPC Magazines Ltd/Robert Harding Syndication; 10–11 Jean-Pierre Godeaut; 12–13 Fritz von der Schulenburg (Jill Barnes-Dacey); 14 Julie Phipps/Arcaid (Antony Sheppard); 15 Nadia Mackenzie; 16 and 17 above left Christian Sarramon; 17 below Simon Brown; 19 Spike Powell/E.W.A.; 20 Marie Claire Maison/Dugied/ Postic; 21 below left Derry Moore; 21 below right Osborne & Little; 22 Marie Claire Maison/Dugied/Postic; 24 Simon Butcher/ Houses & Interiors; 25 above Tim Street-Porter (Designer and owner: Kathryn Ireland); 25 below left Paul Ryan/International Interiors; 25 below right Simon Brown; 26 left Camera Press; 26–7 Geoffrey Frosh (Designed by Stephen Calloway and Oriel Harwood); 27 right Elle Decoration/Dan Lepard; 29 above Michael Dunne/E.W.A.; 29 below Paul Ryan/International Interiors; 30 below left Christian Sarramon; 31 Deidi von Schaewen (Designers: Paul Mathieu & Michael Ray); 32 above Trevor Richards (Timney Fowler); 32–3 above Paul Ryan/International Interiors; 32 below Tim Beddow/E.W.A.; 34 above left IPC Magazines Ltd/Robert Harding Syndication; 34–5 Deidi von Schaewen (Designer: Sylvie Blanchet); 36 above Paul Ryan/International Interiors; 36 below Fritz von der Schulenburg (Julia Boston); 37 Paul Ryan/International Interiors; 38 below left Derry Moore; 38–9 above Agence Top/Roland Beaufre (Chez Gerard Dalmon et Pierre Staudenmeyer – Galerie Neotu, Paris); 39 below left Derry Moore; 40 above David Parmiter/Abode; 40 below left Jerome Darblay; 40 below right Fritz von der Schulenburg (Stephanie Hoppen); 41 Paul Ryan/ International Interiors; 42 above Laura Ashley Ltd; 42–3 below Deidi von Schaewen (Designer: Sylvie Blanchet); 43 above Laura Ashley Ltd; 43 below right Jerome Darblay; 44–5 Christian Sarramon; 45 above Paul Ryan/International Interiors; 45 below right Simon Brown; 50 above Simon McBride; 50 below left Stylograph/Côte Sud/Ingalill Snitt; 50 below right Jean-Pierre Godeaut; 51 Courtesy of Designers Guild, photograph David Montgomery; 54 Fritz von der Schulenburg (Monika Apponyi); 55 above Simon Upton/E.W.A.; 55 below left Fritz von der Schulenburg (Lars Bolander); 55 below right Tom Leighton/E.W.A.; 58 left Courtesy of Designers Guild, photograph by David Montgomery; 59 above right Fritz von der Schulenburg (George Spencer); 59 below left Fritz von der Schulenburg (Stephen Ryan); 59 below right Jean-Pierre Godeaut; 62 above Trevor Richards (Timney Fowler); 62 below left Marie Claire Maison/Dugied/Bayle; 62 below right Marie Claire Maison/Dugied/Postic; 63 above Camera Press; 63 below Agence Top/Pascal Chevallier (Decoration: Christian Badin); 66 left Simon McBride; 66 above right Marie Claire Maison/ Bailhache/Ardouin; 66 below right Marie Claire Maison/Bailhache/Rozensztroch; 67 above Stylograph/Maison Française/Beaud-Cartier; 67 below Camera Press; 70 above Fritz von der Schulenburg (Elgahammar, Sweden); 70 below right Stylograph/Primois; 71 above left Collection La Passementerie Nouvelle, France; 71 below left Jerome Darblay; 71 right Derry Moore; 74 above Fritz von der Schulenburg (Laura Ashley); 74 below left Derry Moore; 74 below right Derry Moore (Nicholas Haslam); 75 above Agence Top/Roland Beaufre (Decoration: Yves Taralon); 75 below Andreas von Einsiedel/E.W.A.; 76 Fritz von der Schulenburg (Colefax & Fowler); 77 below left Paul Ryan/International Interiors; 77 below right Collection La Passementerie Nouvelle, France; 78 below left courtesy of Designers Guild, photograph by David Montgomery; 78 below right Osborne & Little; 79 above Elle Decoration/James Merrell; 79 below Marie Claire Maison/Limbourg/Billaud; 84 Courtesy of Designers Guild, photograph by David Montgomery; 90 Stylograph/Côte Sud/G. de Laubier; 92 Arthur Sanderson and Sons Ltd; 96 above Paul Ryan/International Interiors; 97 Belle; 98 Michael Dunne/E.W.A.; 100 Fritz von der Schulenburg (Laura Ashley); 101 Camera Press; 102 left Agence Top/Pascal Chevallier (Decoration; Françoise Dorget, Paris); 102 right Maire Claire Maison/Dugied/Bayle; 103 Jean-Paul Bonhommet; 104 Fritz von der Schulenburg (Mimmi O'Connell); 105 Derry Moore; 106 Derry Moore; 110 Belle; 113 Laura Ashley Ltd; 114–5 Lars Hallen/Design Press; 116 Walter Smalling Jr; 118 Debi Trelor/Anna Owen/E.W.A.; 123 above IPC Magazines Ltd/ Robert Harding Syndication; 123 below Trevor Richards (Timney Fowler); 125 below Peter Woloszynski; 130 Spike Powell/E.W.A.; 131 Deidi von Schaewen (Designer: Andree Putman); 133 Agence Top/Pascal Chevallier (Decoration: Henri Garnelli, Paris); 138 Laura Ashley Ltd; 139 Jean-Paul Bonhommet; 140 left Agence Top/Pascal Chevallier (Chez l'antiquaire Catherine Arigoni, Paris); 140 right IPC Magazines Ltd/Robert Harding Syndication; 141 left Jean-Paul Bonhommet; 144 Ingalill Snitt; 148 Vogue Living/ Anthony Amos; 149 Marie Claire Maison/Dugied/ Bayle; 152 left Belle; 153 Christian Sarramon; 154 Marie Claire Maison/Dugied/Bayle; 156 Deidi von Schaewen (curtains hand-painted by Claudie & Carine Mandel); 157 Paul Ryan/International Interiors; 158 Fritz von der Schulenburg; 159 Fritz von der Schulenburg (Graham Rust); 160 John Hall; 161 Fritz von der Schulenburg (Barbara Thornhill); 162 Elle Decoration/James Wedge; 163 Vogue Living/Geoff Lung; 164 Deidi von Schaewen (Designer: Fabricio Bruschi; 170 Nadia Mackenzie (Clare Moseley); 171 above Paul Ryan/ International Interiors; 171 below left Fritz von der Schulenburg (Andrew Wadsworth); 175 Colefax & Fowler; 176 Laura Ashley Ltd; 178–9 Jean-Paul Bonhommet.

THE FOLLOWING PHOTOGRAPHS WERE SPECIALLY TAKEN FOR HOMES & GARDENS: 4 below Robin Matthews; 6 below left Jan Baldwin; 6 center right David Parmiter; 17 above right Jan Baldwin; 18 Trevor Richards; 21 above Michael Dunne; 28 above James Merrell; 28 below Henry Bourne; 30 above James Merrell; 30 below right James Merrell; 33 above right James Merrell; 33 below right David Parmiter; 34 below left Trevor Richards; 39 above right Kudos; 46 Robin Matthews; 58–9 above Trevor Richards; 96 below James Merrell; 98–9 Michael Dunne; 120–1 Jan Baldwin; 122 Trevor Richards; 134 James Merrell; 135 Trevor Richards; 141 right James Merrell; 142 Simon Brown; 147 Trevor Richards; 168 James Merrell; 171 below right Jan Baldwin. Thanks to Robert Harding Syndication.

THE FOLLOWING PHOTOGRAPHS WERE SPECIALLY TAKEN FOR CONRAN OCTOPUS: 70 below left, 150 Jan Baldwin (courtesy of John Hardy): 4 above, 6, 8, 127 Nadia Mackenzie (courtesy: Anita Hildreth of George Spencer Decorations): 48–9, 52–3, 56–7, 60–1, 64–5, 68–9, 72–3, 76, 78, 166, 172–4, Michael Newton (styled by Ruth Prentice and Camilla Bambrough); 124, 125 above, 137 Shona Wood (courtesy of Ruth White and Jeffrey Leff); 125 above, 152 right (courtesy of Nadine Bazar).